Journey of a Lightworker

A collection of personal stories from
Lightworkers around the world

Copyright © 2017

All rights reserved.

This book or any portion thereof
may not be reproduced or used
in any manner whatsoever without
the express written permission of
the author except for the use of
brief quotations in a book review.

Printed in Australia
First Printing, 2017
ISBN: 978-0-9945052-8-6

White Light Publishing House
6 Lincoln Way Melton West, VIC,
Australia 3337

www.whitelightpublishingau.com

'Lightworkers are souls who carry the strong inner desire to spread Light – knowledge, freedom and self-love – on earth. They sense this as their mission.

They are often attracted to spirituality and to therapeutic work of some kind. Because of their deeply felt mission, Lightworkers often feel different from other people. By experiencing different kinds of obstacles on their way, life provokes them to find their own unique path.

Lightworkers are nearly always solitary individuals, not fitting into fixed societal structures.'

Jeshua channeled by Pamela Kribbe

*Warriors of light are not perfect.
Their beauty lies in accepting
this fact and still desiring
to grow and to learn.*

Paulo Coelho

Introduction

This book was created for you. You have chosen to read this collection of stories for a reason, and more than likely, you're smiling to yourself right now because you know this is the truth.

You may call yourself a Lightworker, or maybe you're not sure if you're one or not. Perhaps you simply want to know more. Regardless of the point you're at on your journey in this lifetime, you're sure to find the stories inside this book to be inspiring, real, and eerily familiar, as you find that these Lightworker's stories are not so unlike your own.

So, what is a Lightworker, you may ask?

There are so many varying definitions of what it means to be a Lightworker, and all of them will resonate with different people. Essentially though, a Lightworker is someone who has incarnated into this lifetime to help bring light into the world; whether it be via spiritual guidance and healing work, expression through the arts (writing, painting, dancing, singing), humanitarian work, working with children, and the list goes on.

Not all Lightworkers will be found engaging in holistic therapies or psychic work. A Lightworker may be a teacher who encourages children to honour their true selves, a volunteer who gives their time to those in need, or a person who rescues and protects animals. As you can see, Lightworkers are found all across the globe, and are all unique in their own way; just as every soul is.

There are some things that unite all Lightworkers however, and that is light and love. Everything we do is done with love and compassion, with the intention of spreading more light into the world.

Being a Lightworker is not without its challenges, but it is an extremely rewarding role to play during such a significant time of change on earth. Join us, as we explore some of the real stories of Lightworkers from around the world.

Message from
Archangel Metatron

Channelled through Sharon Miralles

To all those Lightworkers, crystal, indigo, rainbow and star children, sensitive souls and empaths – you are children of pure living light and are sent here to heal the Earth. Some of you are angelic helpers who have come to help us in human form. We are in gratitude to you for your loving wisdom and healing on this planet. Archangel Metatron would like to share a message with you to bring you angelic comfort as you journey upon your Earthly mission.

I am Archangel Metatron, devoted servant and bearer of the light of the Creator. I am here at this time to be of service to you and anchor in the ascension energies of pure light and love to you on this planet. Open your heart and receive them joyously. All you need to do at this time is open your heart to love and acceptance. Accept all Beings of the Creator as one and embrace them with love. See all others as not separate from yourself but in union with yourself. Those who create separateness and duality in this world at this time will not ascend to the next level. As Beings of one light, we must live and act in unison. This is the way forward to the next advancement of human consciousness and evolution.

**We light Beings live in a state of love.
Humans live in a world of need and choice.
When you need, ask of it to Heaven in love.
When you choose, always choose
from a place of love.**

Be of service to the light at all times. Expand your consciousness and Divinity through consciously bringing in the light daily into your Being. As light Beings live in a state of permanent love, no negative forces can interfere and penetrate their energy vibration. Earth life is dense and is full of negative energy. Those light workers, crystal, indigo, rainbow and star children, highly sensitive Beings and empaths may be greatly affected at this time on Earth if you are not living in your full light consciousness. You need to be reminded to rest, repair and shed all densities and transmute all frequencies and vibrations back to a state of light. There is nothing wrong with you. You are doing good work even though you remain challenged. You are not alone. The intense energy calls to you now and offers opportunity for further expansion and growth. You are fully supported as long as you remember to turn inwards, rest and recover; release and heal. Situations, events, past memories, relationship issues and inner struggles may all surface even more at this time in order for you to release them. By releasing heavy, burdensome, dense energy, you will allow more light and expanded consciousness to permeate your Being, spiralling your frequencies higher and clearing and opening your heart centre, awakening your Divine potential for a fully expanded heart centre of Divine love – the opening of ascension energies and the beginning of your Cosmic pathway.

This inner journey may not be easy. Those who have awakened will tell you of their struggles. Overcoming these inner struggles and the glorious awakening of the Divinity inside all and the interconnection of all things is the Cosmic gateway to ascension. For many of you on this journey, each experience will be different.

Remember those before you and those of you to come. Bless the past, the present and the future. Through this process, you can expand your DNA and awaken dormant cells by unlocking and freeing yourself from the collective consciousness which has restrained you for so long. Create a new collective consciousness. One of ascension and Beings of light living on Earth in human form while being awakened to the Divine Light in which you are one and will remain always.

To those crystal, rainbow and star children who are fully activated and living in their light, no negative forces on Earth will permeate your energy field as you are protected by your light, your Divinity and by us guardians of the light and love in which we serve. You act as a light bearer, affecting others with a positive charge so great; your work is instrumental on the planet at this time. This is what you have been called here to do. Remain centred and grounded in love and know we are with you. You cannot be distracted from your path and your mission ever. We are with you in love, support, guidance and service at all times. You help your fellow human Beings and Divine souls in immeasurable ways, subtle yet immensely effective.

With love, devotion and in eternal service, Metatron.

With love, light and unity,

Sharon Miralles

Be around the light bringers,
the magic makers,
the world shifters,
the game shakers.

They challenge you,
break you open,
uplift and expand you.

They don't let you play
small with your life.

These heartbeats
are your people.

These people
are your tribe.

Contents

The Healer and the Healed	15
Shining a Light on Self Love	25
Baptised in the Light	37
Unlocking the Door to the Light	57
Trials and Tribulations	69
The Rainbow Journey of an Ascending Seedling	79
Touched by Love	91
Raúl's Angelic Journey	99
Following the Light	113
Not your Stereotypical Lightworker	119
The Spiritual Truth	135
Tale of an Indigo Scout	141
A Little Bit of Heaven on Earth	149
Guided by Love and Light	159
Journey to the Centre of my Soul	165
My Journey	175
Sophialina's Experience	183
The Pathway of the Soul	189
The Journey to Believe	203
Now, I Understand	213
Welcome Back, Light	223

The Healer
and the Healed

By Lani Sharp

I am a born witch. One beautiful warm morning in the February of 1976, a little sunbeam was born – that sunbeam was me! I came forth with magic in me, a born Lightworker you might say. Not only did I arrive in the much-revered Year of the Dragon but I was born on February 2, a sacred day for witches, pagans, wizards, alchemists, magic-weavers, spell-casters and of course Lightworkers of all kinds. In Pagan traditions, in the northern hemisphere, February 2 is known as Imbolc, a time which celebrates the first signs of Spring and the awakening of the light in the Goddess; and in the southern hemisphere where I was born, it is known as Lughnasadh, a time which heralds the first harvest, and the blessings and prosperity this brings with it. I have always had a deep affinity with symbolism, esoterism and mysticism, so being born on this day holds a very special and profound meaning for me and my life's path.

From the moment I took my first breath under the cosmically whimsical cocktail of an Aquarius Sun and Pisces Moon, I was well on my way to healing others.

My father was very sick with terminal and inoperable brain cancer when I was born, having been given only six months to live, but he made a miraculous turnaround after I came bounding into the world, and he lived for another fifteen years, well exceeding the doctors' expectations. I do not take sole credit for this (my dad, after all, was his own healer), however I do feel that a newborn child can literally breathe new life, hope, power and inspiration into a receptive individual. And my dad was the willing and fortunate recipient of this potent life force essence.

Before I share my journey with you, here are a few magical things about me:

- **I am a solitary eclectic witch who casts spells, worships the Sun, wishes on the Moon, basks in the rays of Venus, breathes in Jupiter beams, and can turn anyone into a frog or prince if I so desire.**
- **I am a mother, Lightworker, astrologer, author, tarot reader, crystal healer, numerologist, magician, alchemist, traveller, seeker, teacher, student and dream-believer.**
- **My numerology number is 9, which is a number of vision, compassion, imagination, intuition and holistic perception, stirring one's deepest psychic self and innate healing potential.**
- **My Sun in Aquarius is on the tenth house cusp in my birth horoscope, right on the midheaven, a prominent sign and position pointing me towards the Lightworker's path.**
- **My Moon is in Pisces, giving me a deeply spiritual focus and belief system.**
- **I have every magical tool I need at my disposal, both inner and outer.**
- **I am rich, enriched, loved, loving, abundant and blessed beyond measure.**

- **I am doing what I love every single day and with each breath and step that I take. My lightwork is my passion and I believe that healing others as well as myself is the main reason I was born.**

First and foremost, I am a mother to my precious moonbeam Allira, born under the powerfully Lunar sign of Cancer. She was born in my spiritual home, the tropical Top End of Australia, and we will return there again one day when the time is right. My secondary and biggest passions are astrology and writing: I am a practicing astrologer and published author of 15 books and counting!

My primary aim with all my books is to inspire, encourage, inform, uplift, enliven and of course en–lighten. Writing and sharing my books with the world is all part of my lightwork, and it is my mission to shine light through my words wherever it is needed.

My journey with as and indeed, the Lightworker's path, consciously began when I was seven years old. I was an emotional child, always crying over this or that, feeling other people's sadnesses and tragedies, taking on other peoples' dramas, projections and wounds – you could say I was a typical Lunar Piscean, in that I absorbed everything and everyone around me like a sponge, and became a huge receptacle for emotions. For the most part, I drifted along quite contentedly with the flows and tides of life, but occasionally I would get swept away, caught in a rip or pulled under! And this trouble was compounded by the fact that I was born under an Aquarian Sun, Aquarius being everything that Pisces isn't – Aquarius is detached, alert, rational, intellectual, unemotional and objective, while Pisces is attached, dreamy, irrational, spiritual, emotional and subjective. Herein lay my conflict! Everything I read about Aquarius, to my tender and sensitive seven–year old mind, was a contradiction of who I thought I was and I seemed to be. For a while, I tried to force a persona of a stiff upper lip and stop all the weeping and blubbering over my surroundings. Then one day I had an epiphany: I was reading a book with a title something along the lines of 'Sun Sign/Moon Sign', and realised that there was a life that existed outside of one's star sign, and it was called your Moon sign. Well, what a revelation! Somehow, back in those days before Google, I swiftly discovered my Moon sign: Pisces! I devoured the whole chapter about my Solar/Lunar combination and I must've read it about ten times! How many cups of tea I consumed in this time I will never know (yes, I drank tea when I was seven, did I also mention I was unconventional?) as I was too absorbed and enchanted with the amazing new insights this knowledge provided me about my personality. Suddenly, everything fell into place. I can say that I am still that same exquisite water bearer/fish mix and adore living this experience. I can also say that this momentous moment of crystal clear clarity, is what led me to becoming the Lightworker I am today.

Although I regard myself as a Lightworker and healer, I believe that no one is essentially a healer, except of themselves.

Let me explain. All healing we do can only come from within ourselves. So technically speaking, another person can't 'heal' us – all they can do is provide us with the tools, practices, knowledge, information, or techniques that we can use to heal ourselves. Further, when I provide a healing energy to someone (in the form of passing on knowledge, a tool, a reading, a practice, or a technique), I understand the underlying principle that they are the ultimate healer of themselves and I trust in this concept. If someone asks for a 'healing', I automatically assume and trust that they are receptive to it. And if they are receptive to it, it naturally follows that they will open themselves up to receiving the light they are seeking.

As a Lightworker, I simply provide the tool, channel and/or the information to the recipient and then they do the rest, whether they are aware of this or not. So, if someone walks away from a session or reading feeling somehow still unhealed or broken, then there is something within them that is blocking that healing from taking place and only they can do the necessary work and take the needed steps to begin the healing journey. I am merely the teacher and channel for healing and lightwork.

Remember, healing is an inside job!
No one can heal you but you.

I am simply a channel that can pass this understanding onto you if you request it. Once it is in your hands, then what you choose to do with it is entirely up to you. That is the beauty of being a Lightworker, that I see so many wondrous examples of people healing themselves. They may try to thank me for any insights they have gained, any shifts they can sense or healing they feel has occurred, but I always remind them that they are the primary and ultimate master healer of themselves.

Some principles that I pass onto my clients, friends and family when they have chosen to undertake a healing journey under my guidance are:

- **Love is a Universal vibration that communicates to all species, functions on all levels and expresses our true nature. Love is the foundation of all healing and is the core essence of the life force.**

- **Healing is a skill that can be taught and that grows stronger with practice. Lightworkers and other wellbeing practitioners become stronger at running the energy in their healing ability over time.**

- **The energy follows the natural intelligence of the body to do the necessary work.**

- **Trusting the process is essential. The work may cause temporary pain, emotional issues to arise,**

> or other distressing symptoms – and these are all part of the healing process. The life force and the healing steps work with a complexity and a wisdom that are beyond our conception and levels of comprehension.

- **Everyone is essentially a Lightworker. The ability to assist in healing is natural to all people. Each person's gifts in life and in healing are unique.**
- **No one can really heal anyone else. The person in need of healing is the true healer. The healing practitioner simply holds a resonance to allow the body to heal itself.**
- **It is important to realise that the healing practitioner is also receiving a healing by doing the work.**

And so as a Lightworker, I receive the light myself; as a healer, I receive the healing myself. This is all just part of the nature of the work that I do. I am so blessed to have been given the gift of this very special and unique path. For, although inherent and innate in us all is the capacity for healing others, not that many people choose this journey as their life's work. And that's fine. For this lifetime, they have other things to accomplish, other ways of being and doing that align with their soul's purpose.

I am just grateful that I was born into such a powerful way of life and can offer this gift to others. I was handed the flaming torch when I was born, and will continue to light the path for others who need it, ask for it or have found themselves in the darkness and seek illumination.

In conclusion, many things have happened in my life in the 33 years since I first became a budding astrologer as a tea-drinking seven-year-old seeker. I have died and been reborn a thousand times over, I've shed tears which could fill a river but also smiled a million lines into my face. I have loved, I have lost. I have shattered into pieces and put them all back together. I have been burnt to ashes, I have regenerated. I have been whole and other times I just cannot find the missing piece. I have grown and shrunk, shrivelled and risen.

> **I have been broken, been restored,**
> **had my faith shattered,**
> **had my faith renewed,**
> **become stuck then broke free.**

I have been ever torn between freedom and security, before realising they are one and the same. I have been desperate and I have been at complete utter peace. I have been centered, I have been completely off-course. I have screwed up and been redeemed. I have dwelt in the past, resided in the future and relished the now. I have transgressed and regressed, transcended and sunk back. I have made mistakes and then corrected, been blind and been clear. I have given and received, gone under, jumped over. I have burned bridges and built ones.

> **I have moved mountains and boulders,**
> **yet cried over tiny stones in my shoes.**

I have visited the underworlds, and soared through the sky. I have a vast reservoir of courage that I too rarely tap into. I have surrendered and compromised, doubted myself, lost myself, met myself, knew myself deeply. I have crossed turbulent oceans, yet feared crossing creeks. I have sunk to the bottom, risen to the top, nearly drowned, learned to swim. I have swum against the current and gone with the flow. I have broken through boundaries, and cowered in comfort zones. I have carried and been carried. I have learned the gentle art of discernment between staying put or walking away. I have been defeated, and lost, been a conqueror, and won. I have seen and felt death, and have crumpled with loss.

I have been plagued by doubt and been filled with boundless self-confidence. I have plunged into the unknown, then risen to the light. I tread lightly but ever so deeply. I have pushed boundaries and taken refuge in my soul. I am deeply vulnerable yet courageous beyond measure. I walk the Path and never deviate, for through it all I stay true to myself, my raw, primal, powerful, unshakable self. I have suffered so immensely that the words hurt to write. The scars are deep and raw, some wounds still open. But I am so very proud of all of my battles, the scars, the wounds, and the wisdom they have bestowed. Such is the path of an eternal seeker, a Lightworker.

In essence, I can say what my deepest truths are: I have been enriched by suffering and blessed by adversity. And through it all, I have never given up. And in all this time, along my whole Lightworker's journey, I have never once laid down my life's weapons and tools, because of the biggest and deepest underlying truth of my soul: I was born to do this. And I want more than anything else for someone, even just one soul I may have touched, to say, 'Because of you I didn't give up.' I am in the ever-evolving process of deep and rich healing. And despite – or perhaps because of – everything, I am both the healer and the healed, all at once.

After all, I am a born witch.

So mote it be.

Lani Sharp

Lani is a mother, published author of 15 books, an astrologer with 33 years experience, tarot expert, healer, crystal therapist, teacher of esoteric subjects, passionate spell-caster, ardent dream believer, Lightworker and eternal student of magic, whose spiritual home is in the beautiful tropical north of Australia. She is an accredited member of the World Metaphysical Association, and a member of the Australian Astrologers Federation and Victorian Federation of Astrologers.

Her greatest passions are writing, astrology, reading, esoteric studies, spiritual evolution, personal development and weaving magical spells on behalf of herself and others, using the powers of pure belief, faith, crystals, the cosmos and the Universe.

She wholeheartedly believes that the power of the written word has the potential to transform lives, change the world one page at a time and enhance the mind, body and spirit of everyone who desires it, by creating a sense of deep, timeless and enduring magic.

Find Lani on Facebook:
https://www.facebook.com/luckyastrologybooks

Shining a Light
on Self Love

By Louise Ginglo

Stirring from sleep, I opened my eyes and looked over at where my favourite chair was positioned in the room. It was still dark, so it took me a moment to focus on the area. I remember chills going down my spine as I came to the realisation that something wasn't quite right. I could see an old man dressed in a dark coloured suit, wearing a hat on his head, and he was sitting in my chair. Is he real? I wondered to myself.

The thought of him being real, petrified me, so I pulled the covers up over my head and waited for what felt like forever before taking another look. And when I did, he was still there. He was looking at me; he didn't say or do anything, he was just sitting there. I tried to call out to my parents but I couldn't get my voice to work, so I dove under the covers once again, and when I finally resurfaced, he was gone. That's when I took the opportunity to run out of my room and head straight for my mum and dad's bed.

The next day, when I explained to my mum what I had seen, she told me that I must have had a dream. But, I insisted that I was awake and there really was a man sitting in my chair, looking at me. To this day, I am well aware that my three year old self had seen a spirit. He may have been someone who was connected to me and my family, or he may have previously lived in that house and he just wanted a little visit.

I also know that the reason I was scared and ran out of my room was because I was more scared of the thought that it was a real person sitting in my chair, rather than him being a ghost. This kind of experience is not unusual for me. I have had conversations with loved ones that have passed. I have felt them connect with me by placing their hand on my shoulder, holding my hand or kissing me on my head. I have had visions of weddings, funerals, babies being born, jobs being offered and couples separating, as well as many other things that occur in life. And it happens, while I am awake or asleep.

I knew from a young age that I was different to other people. Not only was it pointed out to me by my own peers that I was odd and that I didn't fit in, but I have always been aware that I have a unique way of sensing the universe and the people in it.

During most of my school years, I was teased a lot about my appearance. So, not only did I feel different about who I was as a person on the inside, I was hugely self-conscious about what I was made up of on the outside.

Feeling unattractive and disliked, I lacked confidence and self-esteem and I was shy and socially awkward.

My first long term relationship, was a massive learning experience for me. I felt so insecure about who I was as a person, I ended up hiding the true me in a secret closet and I threw away the key.

It was easier for me to shun the friends that my boyfriend didn't like, so that I didn't have to listen to him make comments about what they looked like and have him constantly question why I wanted to be friends with these people. I stopped listening to the music I enjoyed and agreed that his music was better. I stopped striving to be a singer because I wasn't talented enough to go anywhere with it. I let my family down by distancing myself from them, because they weren't good enough for him. And, I turned off my unique way of feeling, seeing and hearing as much as I could, it was easier this way. It meant that all I had to focus on was him and what he wanted, instead of feeling for other people. I loved him and he was all I could handle at the time.

**Fortunately for me though,
I always had that little voice
that spoke to me
through the tiny crack
in the door of that secret closet.**

I didn't listen at first, because I was scared of what she had to say. I was worried that she would somehow coerce me into searching for that key and dare me to set the real me free, and then my world as I knew it, would shatter and I wouldn't be able to cope.

**It took years of tears, breakdowns,
falling apart and a heart that had been
broken time and time again, for me to
decide it was finally time to dig deep
and go in search of that key.**

It was no longer good enough for me to put my ear up to that tiny crack in the door and listen to the tiny quiet voice. If I was going to live the life I was born to live, I had to set myself free and allow my authentic voice to come through loud and clear.

I began by getting back into everything I was previously interested in and had pushed aside, such as astrology, numerology, intuitive awareness, mediumship, oracle cards, angels and dream interpretation. I sought guidance from psychics, intuitive counsellors and natural therapists to help me overcome the heartache I had been through and to help me find my way back from hiding in that closet.

Before I knew it, I was making a comeback. I began to receive strong messages in night time dreams, as well as day dreams.

And, I knew it was time to honour my soul by listening to these messages and welcome the guidance I was receiving. I have always known that I am here for a purpose, I just didn't know at the time, what that purpose was.

But, I did know that I was required to continue to evolve and move forward as my authentic self, so that I could discover what it is I am here to do.

After years of working in offices and feeling as though I was suffocating, I was at a loss as to which direction to go next. I applied for an administration job, and even though I could sense that I would hate the role if I were successful in obtaining it, I sent off my resume anyway.

I was called in for an interview and I ended up being offered a position as a Weight Loss Consultant instead. This was something I had never done before, I was intrigued and I jumped at the chance.

This is when I discovered that I love working with people and helping them in a variety of ways.

On the day I started, I was extremely nervous to see my first client. It was even more frightening when the first thing she asked me was 'are you here as my counsellor as well as consulting me on weight loss?' It was obvious she had had a tough week and needed someone to vent to. I politely told her that I wasn't trained to counsel her for other areas of her life, but she talked about it anyway. I was accustomed to people doing this to me at bus stops, in the bathrooms at nightclubs, in a queue at the supermarket or anywhere for that matter, so I sat and listened.

> **As time went on,
> not only was I learning
> a lot about all of my clients,
> I was discovering more
> about me as a person,
> who I am and
> what I am here for.**

I became the consultant that other consultants passed their difficult clients on to. It wasn't because I was a mastermind at getting them to lose their weight, it was because the other consultants labelled me as the patient, even-keeled employee. I was given clients that were considered elderly, others were chronically ill, some had difficult personalities, or an accent that was hard to comprehend. At first, I wondered why these people were passed on to me, but then I realised it was because I was happy to give them the time, the understanding, the empathy and the compassion these amazing people needed, as well as my yearning to help them as best as I could. I was blessed to make a connection with each of these clients and they all taught me something valuable along the way.

While other consultants rolled their eyes in frustration, or talked about how strange these people were, or became impatient with the time it took to work with them, I was learning about accepting people as they are, recognising the beauty they each possessed and welcoming them with no judgement. Helping these clients made me happy.

If they were able to walk out of their consultation with a smile on their face and feel that the words they spoke were heard, and that they were worthy of having time spent on them, and they felt inspired to keep moving forward and motivated to live in the healthiest way possible, then I was happy to guide them to feeling that way. And in turn, these people inspired me to dive further into myself and work on improving on everything that I have to offer.

At this point in time, I didn't think of myself as a Lightworker. All I knew was that I felt the intense need to help other people feel good about themselves and to be compassionate and kind to themselves.

Working with people and hearing their individual stories allowed me to take an interest in where people come from and how they have come to be the way they are.

As a consultant I sat and listened to clients and I took in every word they would use to describe themselves. I felt their disappointment, their sadness, their frustration and anger and it was all aimed at their own being. Most of them didn't reach the goal they set out to achieve because they didn't believe in themselves, they couldn't see how incredible and beautiful they were, whether they were overweight or not. And it dawned on me that this was how I talked about myself and how I felt about myself too. I was just like my clients.

As someone who had battled with my own weight loss and image problems, I became inspired to approach it from a new perspective. Instead of constantly focusing on losing weight, I began to look at ways to lead a healthier lifestyle.

**With this, came the need
to accept my flaws
and be proud of
my positive attributes.**

And while doing this, I figured out that it was important to learn to love the fuller version of me, instead of waiting to meet the imaginary thinner version of me; the person I once believed was going to be more outgoing, happier and more confident once I had lost weight.

Leading a healthy lifestyle and recognising the benefits of being healthier took me on a journey to falling in love with me, on the inside and out.

**My self-love has made a massive
difference to how I approach
certain situations in my life.**

So much so, that I came to understand that guiding others to loving who they are so that they can reap the benefits of self-love is part of my work as a Lightworker.

After leaving the weight loss industry to look after my children, I was looking for avenues to help people that were struggling with their weight and their image. After taking on some extra study and learning a little more about weight management and nutrition, I was guided to begin the process of writing.

**I believe that my gift for writing
is providing me the opportunity
to communicate with people
in an emotional and heartfelt way.**

I am able to reach people in more ways than I could if I were to rely solely on face to face consultations. The reader is able to relate to what I have written and feel as though I am writing about them. The short stories that I am called to write, contain inspirational and channelled messages about believing in yourself, lessening self-doubt, finding strength in who you are, letting go of limitations, learning to say good-bye to negativity, embracing a positive well-balanced life, being mindful and staying present, seeing the bigger picture and of course, learning to love yourself.

> **Every time I write a new story,
> I am aware that I am
> tapping into what people
> need to read on that day.**

Whenever I post a new piece through Facebook, I often receive private messages or comments from people saying that they can relate to that story. They tell me that they are experiencing what was happening within that story and are grateful to receive a positive message that is honest, yet full of love, hope and healing.

I love writing. I feel completely comfortable communicating my messages in this way. And, I am aware that I have many other stories to create, ones that will heal, inspire and touch people's hearts, because this is what I am here to do.

Helping people to weigh less physically is just one branch on my tree of life journey and writing inspirational and healing words is another. I also have an even bigger vision of what my life-purpose as a Lightworker is going to be. I have created the name of my business, Weigh Less Sanctuary. I see this as a relaxing environment for people to come into, a place where they can experience many ways to weigh less in body, mind and spirit. I envisage intuitive consultations, group sessions and workshops, as well as many other tools and soothing ways to walk away feeling loved, lighter and brighter. This dream hasn't yet been realised, but every time I imagine it happening, I feel butterflies in my stomach; it excites me, and I am confident it will come to fruition.

As a Lightworker, I don't see the world as black and white. I feel everything with intense sensitivity. I hear hidden sounds and whispers. I inhale the scent of the universe and get happily drunk on the sweetness, the earthiness, the muskiness and the woodiness of nature. I see the dark and colourful sides to every event, story, drama and person.

The advantage of seeing the many sides to an issue, a problem, a fight, an argument, a bad situation and a good situation, means that I can understand the many roads that have led to, and then away from the core of what has happened or is occurring. I am able to give light to situations by going through the many reasons as to why someone reacted in a certain way or why someone is going through something they can't understand. I am able to give people food for thought.

Friends, family and clients have often responded by saying, 'oh, I never thought of it in that way. You have a way of always putting things into perspective for me.'

The downside to this though, is if someone isn't open to seeing another side to the story, they will see me as condoning or defending a person who has done something wrong or unforgivable. This isn't the case. For me, it's about choosing love, compassion and empathy over hate, anger and judgement.

To me, there is nothing better than helping people to feel better in their life, whether it's via consultation, writing an inspirational story or just listening to someone who needed to be heard and lifting their spirits by being there for them.

So what happens when I am in need of a shoulder to cry on or someone to lift my spirits and reassure me that I am on the right track and all will be okay? For me, it's about having other Lightworkers in my life.

Some of them I seek out and book an appointment, so that this is my time to receive help in any way I need. I have also connected with many other Lightworkers who are providing daily help and assistance on social media and their messages and guidance are warmly invited. I also have friends who are

Lightworkers, some I get to have coffee and lunch with on a regular basis, while others I haven't physically met yet, but I know they are a phone call, email or private message away, and I am extremely grateful for all of these connections.

I also find that if I am battling with self-doubt, fear, anxiety and feeling low, a feather will appear before me, a butterfly will flutter near me, a dragonfly will hover at my feet and unicorns make themselves present in dreams, meditations, oracle/guidance cards and stunning images in random places.

All of these connections, messages and signs remind me that I am being guided by a divine light and I am being protected, embraced and deeply loved.

Shining my light is what I do on a daily basis. It's not just reserved for clients who pay for an appointment. And I know this is the case for all Lightworkers.

I am completely awake and aware to the fact that I will continue to find more ways to help people through my writing, via intuitive consultations and by providing a safe, welcoming space for people from all walks of life to weigh less in their own life. And, I will continue to shine my light and gently guide others to discover an abundance of self-love.

'When we connect, the light becomes even brighter and will shine on the path that will lead you towards that radiating glow within. Coming face to face with that shimmering light, your true beauty will appear and you will fall in love with your brilliance, your uniqueness and the gorgeous human being that you are.'

Channelled message — Louise Ginglo

Louise Ginglo

Louise is an Author and Weigh Less Consultant. Louise has contributed written pieces to books such as, Writing: The Powerful Healer and Inspiration Bible. Her self-published book Conversations With My Reflection guides her readers into leading a healthy balanced lifestyle and discovering self-love through inner reflection.

As a writer, Louise creates inspirational stories channelled through her intuition. Using compassion, love and empathy, Louise has the innate ability to connect with others through her work. Her readers are able to relate to the stories, reflect on the messages within the context and discover peace and healing through what they have read. Louise obtained her Weight Loss Consultant Diploma through the Australian College of Weight Management.

With a deep understanding of what it is like to struggle with weight and body-image issues, Louise employs a gentle, realistic and down-to-earth approach to helping others on their weigh less journey.

You can follow Louise, or contact her via her Facebook page:
www.facebook.com/weighlesssanctuary

Baptised in
the Light

By Jacquelene Close Moore

I n the moment I became aware that I had stopped breathing, I stopped struggling and I sank deeper and deeper down. Everything had gone from sky blue, to aquamarine, to azure, to cobalt, then to deeper blues until everything was an inky indigo, and then, finally, black.

I was only five and a half years old and had just drowned in my parents' back yard swimming pool. I had fought for air, struggled to try to swim, and was now strangely blissful, and relieved of that mortal existence. I travelled along a dark tunnel, and then out into a brilliant bright white light. Then finally, out towards a beautiful garden. In this place I was calm, there were roses everywhere and the sky and atmosphere was overlaid with a light, golden hue. I walked over the small bridge and stepped into the garden where an elderly couple stood waiting to welcome me.

'What the hell was that life about?' I demanded. 'I went there to teach peace and love. That was anything but peace and love. I don't understand!' With deep compassion, understanding and a wry smile on both faces, they looked at each other and replied, 'How can you hope to teach what you have not had to find within yourself?'

Like a tonne of bricks landing on my head, the realisation of the gravity of my soul's purpose in this life hit my human awareness.

My eternal soul, which was of course a lot older than my five-and-a-half-year-old human brain, understood it all too well. The rest of me didn't yet comprehend it and was back on the earthly plane, floating face down in the chlorinated water of the swimming pool in my parents back yard. My human child brain would need a lot longer to process all of this information, it would take many years to come to terms with it. IF I decided to return that is.

I do recall looking back and forth at times during my experience on the other side, although it was a hazy kind of awareness.

It is somewhat patchy these days as an adult recounting it. I recall seeing the swimming pool from a great height, my frantic mother, the ambulance workers, and at some point later, momentarily being back in my body in what felt like warm water. I heard a woman's voice talking to my mother saying, 'We have her back!' My consciousness began slipping away again and I could hear the shaking in that same unknown woman's voice calling out, 'We're losing her again!' Her voice became more distant and then was gone. I returned to the garden on the other side for an unknown amount of time.

**Whilst part of me remained
in that otherworldly place,
I was later told that for two days,
my unconscious body
lay in a hospital bed in a room
shared with a seventy-year-old doctor.**

He was in the bed next to mine and was also not expected to survive. He'd had a heart attack, and lingered for the duration of my mother's vigil as she sat beside my bed praying for my return. Meanwhile in the rose garden, I wondered who the two elderly people were that I was talking in great depth to. They looked familiar, but I just wasn't sure. They told me that their identity wasn't as important as was the key decision for me; whether I wanted to go back to my life and continue with my soul's purpose of being in that life, or not.

**They showed me aspects of the life
I was yet to live well in advance.**

They explained that it would be very hard as I grew up, but that they would help me as much as they could. They showed me many of the people I was yet to meet, experiences I would have; the good, the bad and the ugly. They explained to me how all experiences, whether we see it as good or bad can be just as rich in what it offers us. They also told of how we incorporate it all into the tapestry that forms our later wisdom and the sense of peace we can bring to our life, and that of others, entirely by our own attitude and approach. They showed me my first husband, and also certain relatives of my second husband. At the time, I didn't quite understand; surely marriage was for a lifetime! I didn't believe in making promises without keeping them, yet it all makes perfect sense now, over 39 years later.

Finally, when the prospect of husbands didn't do it for me, they offered for the door between heaven and earth to remain open for me if I went back. They explained that instead of me having to die again in order to return to this place, I would be able to spend my earthly life walking between the two worlds.

> **They said that whenever the earthly world got too exhausting, I could take refuge for a time on the other side, return, and keep moving forward in my life.**

That was the one thing that made me finally agree to return to this life, knowing I had a place of refuge. The job I had taken on in this life seemed immense and I knew I would need some form of retreat.

Meanwhile back on earth, moments before I woke up in my hospital bed, the seventy-year-old doctor who shared the same room, turned to face my mother and passionately uttered his last words ... 'You know, I really wanted to live!' He exhaled his last breath, and remained, facing my mother in quite literally a dead stare at her. He had expressed to her that he had been afraid of dying. Almost immediately after he passed, I returned from my dormant state.

> **I glared at my mother and said, 'You know, I really didn't want to come back!'**

That was really awful to say, especially as the only child to a mother who desperately wanted children, a mother who had six miscarriages before me, and was never able to have another child again after me. Unlike my doctor friend, who seemed not quite ready to die, it seemed in contrast, I was not quite ready to live.

> **I spent many years following that incident, fearing life and living. But I never feared death.**

Much of my childhood was spent fighting one illness or another; asthma, flu after flu, bronchitis, pleurisy, pneumonia and so on. I remembered waking at times and half seeing the doctor through my blurred vision, with eyes that I could barely keep open and hearing my grandmother talking. At one point I recall hearing her questioning the doctor whether I would make it through the night. Many times I was made to sleep half sitting up in a warm room, with furniture positioned to cut out cold drafts from windows or nearby doors. Over time I became more resilient, and my grandfather and grandmother would sit with me. We would read our tea leaves and grandpa would also read my palms from time to time.

Whilst visiting my father at one point, he took me out to the back yard, past the very same swimming pool in which I had drowned; at that house where I no longer resided. He said he wanted me to play a game of hide and seek. He made me stand at the back fence and count to 100 before coming to find him. He explained that he might be anywhere, down the street, in the car, in the house, next door, at the milk bar; anywhere. He told me once I had finished counting to 100, I was to come straight to him, no matter where I thought he was; and find him.

I asked him why he was making me do this but he wouldn't explain. He simply made me face the fence and count. When I had reached 100, I went directly to the back door, walked through the kitchen, straight up the hallway and stopped at the door of the front bedroom. I stood there in front of an old, olive winged back velvet recliner chair. I called out, 'Daddy, I have found you, can you come out from behind that chair please.'

**There was complete silence,
not even the sound of breathing to guide me.
I was only guided by one sense;
the feeling that had drawn me
straight towards him.**

I started becoming anxious, and called out to him a number of times with no response. I felt uncomfortable about walking around the back of the chair for some reason, and felt it was better if I made him come out from behind the chair on his own. I didn't realise it then, but the anxiety I was feeling was not my own, it was his. How could his daughter find him this way, so quickly? What else could she do? How should he handle his own empathic tendencies in such a challenging and not all that supportive world for people such as us?

As he stood up, I saw his beautiful, emerald green aura surrounding him as he half whispered. 'How did you find me?' He was as pale as a sheet. 'I can see your colours daddy, you're such a beautiful green!' He stuttered out the words, 'What colours are you talking about?' 'The colours around you daddy.' His emerald green aura rapidly turned a bright shade of tomato as his complexion went even whiter than I thought possible. 'What did I do wrong daddy?' I cried. I didn't understand back then that his red aura wasn't anger, it was fear. 'How did you do that?' He mouthed.

I gave him the same reply I would later repeat to him as an adult; when I was to find him again, only this time across the other side of Australia.

I said, 'You are my daddy, and I am your daughter. I will always be able to find you; but only for as long as you want me to.'

His expression changed to the fear that matched his aura. He scolded me,

'Don't tell anyone you can do this!'

As he said that I, saw the image in his mind of men in white coats and a small white van carrying someone away. He concluded verbally, 'They will come and get you if you do.'

So, for a number of years, I remained silent about my gifts. It was safer that way. Other children didn't see what I saw, didn't feel what I felt, didn't hear what I could hear, and they didn't know what I knew. I spent my childhood having 'normal' conversations with school friends and often when I wasn't with them, I spent time with a number of different teachers in spirit. They were the ones I could ask to receive help and guidance from when I couldn't ask many of the living as they wouldn't be likely to understand.

As is normal for most, puberty appeared in early high school. I found my gifts exposed in the most embarrassing and undeniable way in the middle of the classroom. On this particular day, I went into a trance, channelling in front of other students. When I 'came to' they were shocked and speechless for the first time since I had known them.

I became the weird kid, or maybe I already was. In a country town, it was even worse to be weird, especially if you were also 'spooky'.

I remember another episode after we moved back to the city. This time in library study group; you know where you are expected to be really quiet. I found myself involuntarily standing all of a sudden with one arm up, elbow bent, the other arm down, while correctly and involuntarily predicting the next year's federal election results. I talked about the 'recession we had to have' before the words were ever used in the media. When I regained control of my body and being that day, I found myself standing there in front of many seated, shocked fellow students, and an equally stunned teacher. None of whom knew quite how to take me, so said nothing. I didn't know how to take myself at that point, and we all must have silently agreed to say nothing and pretend it didn't happen. Everyone resumed their reading and referencing and I may as well have called out something as unremarkable as 'Lovely day isn't it?' instead.

I tried to have a normal job, a normal life and find my place in the real world when I left school, despite my calling doing a lot of calling to me.

I desperately wanted anything and everything normal and human because all of this seemed too hard, too frightening, and too much.

How could I handle the responsibility of helping people in their lives when my own life was still so ungrounded? What did I possibly know that would help anyone? I was still so afraid of others, of myself and of life itself. I had a lot of discovery to do, and a lot of unpacking. But it was when my grandfather died that I finally better understood the two people who had helped me from the other side while I was in my near death experience as a young child, and I got down to work not long after his passing. Before I began my work I performed a ritual of dedication of the remainder of my life to the work of spirit.

I sat and wrote down my code of ethics and have expanded upon it since, as a helpful additional guide to help me remain centred and focused on what my work is all about.

I later realised that when my grandfather died, he resembled the man on the other side who had spoken to me in the rose garden. Less than two years later, when my grandmother passed, she had changed to look exactly as she had on the other side standing next to him, as she had when I had been there in that timeless space, where the past, present, and future were all converging at once. The two people on the other side who helped me decide to return had been my grandfather and grandmother. When they passed from this life, I was in my early twenties, they now looked the same as they had almost 20 years before; after my near death experience.

At times, my journey has required absolute forgiveness but never forgetting and always complete faith.

At other times, it has taken a great deal of sacrifice personally and financially. It has required me to involve myself in community efforts and give to charity, to sometimes take great risks, to be absolutely direct and unflinching in the reinforcement of my own worth and boundaries. I have gone throughout the journey towards my self-discovery, self-healing, and expanded my development to always challenge myself that bit more in order to help others.

If you were to ask me what else I would do if I wasn't doing this work, I could not tell you. This is who, how, why, and what I am.

I entered further psychic development training as an adult. Not so much to develop a connection to my psychic, intuitive and mediumistic abilities, but to learn how to manage all of the sensory input from people and without picking up too much about every single person I passed by in the supermarket. I also had to learn to communicate what I saw, felt, heard, smelt, and was experiencing on behalf of people in a way that could help them without being too confronting. I feared the responsibility, I was terrified of public speaking, afraid of radio interviews, and most of all I didn't want to get it wrong for people. I ended up fighting off extreme nerves and doing live public readings and demonstrations for some of Australia's most prestigious companies. I have a live weekly worldwide psychic radio show on a USA based radio station with a growing audience of over one million. I have met many famous people which has taken me out of my once shy and afraid state, to coming into my full potential and being someone who is unashamedly creative. I don't care who sees me authentically dancing, living, and breathing with passion.

We are all capable of great things if we open to our authenticity with drive.

Many years ago I also foresaw myself on the cover of a magazine; fifteen years ahead of it actually happening. At the time I thought perhaps I was having an ego attack or delusions of grandeur. The part of me that knew it would one day be true shuddered at how 'un-ready' and unprepared I felt. I had fifteen years to catch up and no actual desire to enter that space. I had started writing in addition to painting and drawing my visions from spirit as it has always felt important to share the messages I receive. While I never pushed for the things I felt would happen, I kept gently going in the direction I felt deeply guided toward.

I spent years working with different teachers in spirit as well as by living teachers who approached me along the way. I also did a great deal of paid training.

> **To me, your advancement in your work with spirit is similar to sand.**
> **If you open your hand and scoop sand into it, much of it remains in your palms and some of it inevitably flows through your fingers.**
>
> **If you try to close your fist tightly around the sand, much of it rushes between your fingers and you keep far less of it. Just like sand, spirit reacts better to the energy of those who don't seek to control or hold it just for themselves.**

It responds best to those who seek to allow it to flow and be in a cooperative creation with openness.

All of my teachers touched my life in so many ways. For six months I had daily lessons from the other side with an interesting man who refused to tell me who he was until we finished the 'course' he was giving me. He shared his knowledge about counselling techniques, what the shadow self was, and how to confront one's own shadow in a helpful manner. He taught me about duality, symbolism, and how to become whole with oneself and see oneself in the mirror of others.

At the conclusion of the day he declared as his last day of training me, he said he would now show me who he was, and asked that I drive to a certain library two suburbs over from our home at the time. It was a library I had never been to before. He showed me where the library was and where to park. He then walked ahead of me through the front door of the library and down an aisle. When I caught up to him, he asked me to pick up 'that' book from the top shelf 'up there'. He spoke in his usual, thick accent. I reached up on tippie-toes and brought down a book with a photo of him on the cover.

I almost stopped breathing, he was Carl Gustav Jung.

He said 'See! See what happens when you ask for proof? You should always ask for proof, Jacquelene. Now I really had better go. You have the books now, so you don't really need me to be here anymore.' I stood there in shock for some time before leaving that library.

I have had many other spirit visitors, from animal guides and totems, a group of ascended masters, the angels, spirit from many cultures, and deities that I have accurately described and named for my Indian clients only to find that is the exact deity their family has had a strong devotee connection with for two hundred or more years.

I also have one very enthusiastic Traditional Chinese Medicine Teacher who was rather frustrated after spending six months with me daily. When he concluded our 'training,' I refused his request to 'return' to Chinese Medicine practice 'again'. I hadn't known that there was any pre-existing contra-deal in this life, but said he would see me ten years after that. Sure enough, when I finally overcame my fear of needles by having acupuncture, he did see me again, to the exact year of his promise to do so. He would often pop in on acupuncture sessions and instruct me to tell the doctor where to put the needles. He still does to this day, but we have a better understanding these days; and I do work in conjunction with Traditional Chinese Doctors at times for clients. He kept his word to me about seeing me again in many ways. People who share his family name fly their family to Australia from China to consult me at times.

Just as many families from Shanghai and Nanjing have also found their way to me. Some have adopted me in a way, and when I have heard traditional songs sung to me from that region I have involuntarily cried tears of recognition.

I used to call my Chinese Doctor teacher in spirit 'Ling from Nanjing,' but actually his name is Li Shezhen. He was indeed from Nanjing when he lived; in that time, one would travel through Shanghai to get to Nanjing when you travelled from the coast. For me, the journey between these two cities represents a well-worn path.

At times Li Shezhen still does a special kind of acupuncture from the other side on me, and sometimes on my clients. When he visits me, he often tells me that time is precious and always seems to be in a rush.

I guess being busy is a good problem to have and I have been blessed with the same issue. Often we draw spirits to guide us that share similar or same attitudes and life experiences.

I recall entering a medical terminology course and on the first night, despite never having studied Latin, nor medicine, nor medical terminology, I was able to decode all of the medical terms into what they meant inexplicably that night; despite it being the first night of a six-week course. But then, with a life spent with doctors in spirit and in person, it has to have some additional benefits. I find that I can often see what is happening in the client's wellbeing. I use the five element theory, and can see the colours of the elements of spirit and nature when working with clients, although this is not the sole focus of my work.

> **My work is to help people**
> **find peace and the love**
> **that is within themselves.**
> **Sometimes that means showing them**
> **a range of things, from wellbeing,**
> **to the course of their life**
> **and how to get more out of it.**

I have many other special beings who have visited me and helped me. To this day, I feel humbled by what they have all shared with me. I always ask for proof in my work. I find seeking confirmation to be one of the best ways to retain my trust in my work and stay on track with my visions.

> **Whilst being honest with yourself**
> **is the second most important tool**
> **for psychic development after wanting**
> **to help others, you cannot always guarantee**
> **that the person who seeks your visions**
> **will be honest with themselves or with you.**

They may not be completely open to the help you offer them. This is why trusting what you get is so important, as much as being prepared to say no sometimes. It is vital to be able to communicate it all in a harmonious, confident and nurturing manner as much as possible. Humans are naturally conflicted beings; they often don't say what they feel in their heart and often don't feel in their heart what they say. A good reading can break through that conflict most of the time, but not always.

Being a good reader means knowing that you never will stop learning and having a good understanding of how far you can open 'that door' and when you cannot.

Since 1995, I have appeared on radio, television, in print and digital media. I have done well over 15,000 readings for clients in over 80 countries. These readings have been on everything from love, relationships, career, finances, spiritual direction, businesses and other people's own psychic development. I have had clients from all walks of life from international students who say I am like their mom, to parents, teachers and psychologists. I have read for lawyers, accountants, celebrities, athletes, artists and other psychics.

Some people have been ready to hear the message, others have tried to deny the message only to confirm it in their next sentences.

Yet others have asked me why, when other psychics tell them they are psychic, I didn't tell them they were psychic. They seem surprised when I hand them the note paper I wrote on and folded up when they first sat down at the start of the reading; I have gotten them to open up the note and read something like, 'Why, when other psychics tell me I am psychic didn't you tell me I am psychic?' Or I repeat the exact words they asked their friend and name the wine they don't want me to know they drank before coming to see me.

Often it is much more poignant things that I pick up, like which song they wished they could have played at their sibling's funeral, and that they didn't choose it because it would have made them cry too much.

Many are surprised when I tell them exactly what pattern is holding them back from real progress in their life. At times it has been what the issues are in a relationship that they later are thankful I pointed out. Sometimes I tell them the exact sale price of their home, at times I have helped on missing person's cases, some of which have been very high profile. I will never name those cases, because for me it is about creating peace in people's lives, especially the family of the missing person. For me, this means not adding to public speculation and respecting the dignity of the missing or deceased and their family. Another reason I do mediumship in private readings and not on stage is that in medium readings I can go to deep places and at times experience the broken collar bone or other events the passed over loved one had in life as a confirmation point of proof of their connecting in with me. In stage readings I cannot afford to go into that energy and instead bring out things about people in the audience and their life in a way that is accurate but positive, and light.

Honouring how ready or unready someone is for their truth and doing so in an uplifting way is the key element for me in being able to read for them. It helps me remain effective as a fulltime professional in this field after 21 years. In life the thing that causes the most strife for people, is when they aren't able to appreciate what they have.

Anxiety is often derived when people fear that they aren't where they think they should be, refuse to accept things as they are, and when they compare their low lights to other people's highlights, or are jealous of other peoples' success.

It is a fear of lack or of missing out. At times they want the thing or things they don't have and forget to appreciate what they do, or can have. So often, wealthy people just want to find someone who truly loves them, regardless of their wealth. Gratitude for what you do have can make you rich in spirit, no matter your bank balance. If you are poor, you won't become rich by hating those who are.

I guide people toward understanding that by loving what you do, doing it well, and focusing on being thankful for what you have, you are more likely to find happiness and indeed will help you become rich in spirit.

I treat the dawn of each new day as a new beginning, a new opportunity to live again, to make today the best day so far. I see each new day as the beginning of the rest of my life. Because of that I can work a 20-hour day at times, both in appointments and in writing pieces like this. Fuelled by purpose, driven by a desire to do and be better, to share with you something that may spark your own inspiration and drive to be all you can be.

While I'm alive, I am going to live this life with every breath, with every drop of my sweat, with every ounce of my being; and with every beat of the heart that is still functioning long after the passing of that doctor in the bed next to the child me. A man who, like I do now, felt a great deal of purpose, felt he had so much more to do and to offer the world. I get to continue where he left off; and because of him and so many teachers besides him, I am reminded to aspire to be my best and make the most and more from what life gave me and to share it with ever soul I meet. I see it all as a win in my own personal race with me. Winning is not about others losing, it is not about passing the finishing line first.

It is about doing all you can with what life presents to you, about never giving up and not compromising on your authenticity. If you do fall down, if you aren't at your personal best at some stage, get back up, make sure you learn what you can from it, move forward and keep going.

I use and highly recommend daily activities to help you calibrate and recalibrate your senses. This is especially important if you are an empath and have just dealt with your opposite, a narcissist or sociopath. Narcissists and sociopaths can make empaths question their skill and sanity after the narcissist's favourite activity of gas-lighting you. I suggest clearing your energy and not beating yourself up after such an exchange.

Recalibrating your energy regularly helps you fend off self-doubt and overcome challenges to your correct insight, and to grow beyond any incorrect interpretations of the true nature of the messages you receive.

If you use every day things and events to recalibrate, you gain confirmation a lot faster and this will help you know you're still on track and help you regain your confidence more quickly. Use everything, from how long you feel something will take at the shop, what you feel the actor will say next on a show you haven't seen before, what you feel the car in front of you will do next in traffic, and whether you need to switch lanes. You can also use your skills to detect which fruit and vegetables are actually fresh, and in what way. You can check which supplements contain what is says on the label and at what percentage. You can also sense the amount on bills in the post before opening the envelope.

I also ascribe to the old saying 'Before enlightenment, chop wood, carry water, after enlightenment, chop wood carry water.'

Beginners should be aware that you really need to prepare your energy with daily meditation to prime yourself before expanding your psychic awareness so that you grow in a way that is safe, positive, and constructive.

It is also helpful to seek balance in your day to day life rather than trying to seek 24/7 'amazeballs' spirit experiences. Don't do yourself and your teacher the disrespect of enrolling in a year-long psychic development class, then go off and spend numerous weekends away at workshops elsewhere and not do the homework they set. Focus, consistency, and dedication is fundamental to excellent results. The level of focus you apply to your training will reflect in your eventual results in readings and in the field. Like all muscles in a work-out program, it is as much about the rest you have away from and in between psychic exercise as the weights you pump. It is no good just working out the one area of your being. You can balance your psychic and intuitive gifts by doing plenty of 'normal' things in between exercises. Journaling your psychic visions and later correlating it with outcomes also gives you the opportunity to test yourself out. If you are tuned in correctly, these exercises become a page by page body of evidence of your correct predictions and psychic experiences.

The thing to remember as you develop, help others, and make your way in the world is that not everyone is going to love you, be supportive, or even be happy for you.

And that this is perfectly okay, you aren't the message anyway. They don't have to like you and you don't have to resonate with them. It isn't a competition. Some people you will never have met will make all sorts of weird assumptions and judgements about you, much of which will be based on their view of themselves rather than a true reflection of your character and nature. So, go where you feel supported and safe. At times, go well beyond your comfort zone when you feel guided to do so.

**Always seek to do your best,
ignore false put downs as much
as you should discern
and ignore false compliments,
and always seek your own proof.**

When you gain proof, take note of it, don't demand 70,000 other forms of the same proof about the same event; spirit is patient, but not that patient.

Although I ran in the opposite direction of my work for years, it kept finding me. If you are meant to work in this field, it will always find you. Whilst many are called, few are chosen because in the end it is down to you choosing whether or not to follow your calling. May you travel well,

With love, Jacquelene Close Moore

Jacquelene Close Moore

Jacquelene is based in Melbourne Australia and travels Australia wide and internationally with her work.

Jacquelene presents Soul Star Radio, a live worldwide psychic show broadcast via USA based A1R Psychic Radio, a network with a growing audience of over one million listeners globally.

Jacquelene is the sixth generation of psychics in her family. And is a psychic, medium, empath, and connected to all the senses. She has completed over 15,000 readings for clients from over 80 countries around the world since 1995. First ever awarded Psychic of the year Victoria 2004, Psychic Ambassador 2013, Jacquelene has appeared and read for audiences at some of Australia's most prestigious companies and events and is available for one to one private readings, media appearances, and corporate, group bookings Australia wide and internationally.

www.Jacquelene.com.au
www.Facebook/Jacquelene.com.au

Unlocking the Door
to the Light

By Ann Hannon Hughes

A Lightworker seeks to bring love, harmony and healing to planet earth. By sharing their natural gifts with others, more and more people will come out of the darkness and into the light. Darkness is fear based and the light is all love. A Lightworker undertook this role before they were born, although it may take a while to become aware of their gifts. They can be found in any walk of life, as their gifts can be varied, but their common purpose is to shine light and share love in all its variations with mankind. Their combined goal is to raise the vibration of planet earth to a place of understanding, compassion and love which will ultimately lead to peace.

The light is creation itself. The energy or being that created everything from the planets to the grain of sand on a beach is light energy. It permeates in and around everything, and all living things upon the earth are alive because of it. We may call it God, the Divine, the Source, the All–That–Is, but this is the same light energy being we are referring to. Without rules and regulations, it just is. The tiny bit of the Creator that is ours is sometimes referred to as the soul and it is here that all the qualities of the Creator are found.

**We are born in light,
but once we start to experience life,
influenced by human, social and
environmental conditions, our light can
get hidden by negative circumstances,
which can be seen as darkness.**

Negative thoughts, illness, toxic relationships, defeatism, all things that are in complete contrast to the light can be seen as darkness. To overcome the darkness, the soul draws experiences to its human host which give them opportunities to grow in light and disperse some or all of the darkness, but on an intellectual level, the human doesn't recognise this and sees the challenge as more darkness ascending upon them.

**A Lightworker can, through their
personal gifts received from the light source,
inspire or guide others to find their light.
They can help light
the way out of the darkness.**

I was born and raised in England to Irish parents, who left Ireland as young adults for more favourable economic shores. I had a happy childhood and other than some odd dreams and strange memories, it was a typical childhood growing up in an Irish home with lots of fun, music and dancing. After completing my education, I started a career in law, working mainly in the area of family law and domestic violence. After meeting and marrying my husband, we left England and came to live in Ireland. We decided that Ireland would provide a better environment for bringing up children, particularly in rural Ireland which is where we finally settled. I have two beautiful daughters, who are now young women, both studying at university. I was widowed 10 years ago, while my children were quite young. I was always a stay-at- home mom and when my youngest daughter started school, I also started working at the school as librarian and school secretary. After my husband died, I began working in the school as a special education needs assistant.

I was always a seeker of knowledge, both factual and mystical.

The mystical arts fascinated me from my teens, and although not popular in those days, I used to seek out books to learn more. Books have been a major part of my life, reading from a very young age, and they were also an important part of my spiritual journey.

Living in Ireland gave me more time to spend reading. I read books about ancient Egypt and other ancient civilisations and I was fascinated. I would devour the new knowledge and I wanted to know more and more about life from the beginning of time.

Raised a Catholic, I was used to praying but now I started to ask more. I wanted to know everything. I wanted to know God.

So, my journey began.

Intuitively, I was led and drawn to certain books, and each book I read seemed perfect for what I was currently asking. It felt, on a deeper level, that the books were choosing me and as well as receiving so much knowledge, both through books and intuitively, later through meditation practice, I was forming a relationship with God, the source of all that is, and I have moved with this all-knowing, all-watching, all-loving presence ever since. That was over 20 years ago, and my journey has been quite amazing.

Through meditation and contemplation, I was receiving guidance. When challenges came, I became calmer and less reactive. While in a calmer frame of mind, I was able to understand the lessons contained in these challenges and once I accepted that the challenge had purpose, I found I could work through them more easily.

The death of a loved one is probably the biggest challenge most of us will face.

My dad was the first of the people I loved to pass away and I hurt so deeply. I thought my dad was too young to die at 69 and my mom was broken without him. Their plans for retirement were shattered, just like that! By that time, I had a loving presence continually with me and was already working with angels in my life, but I hurt so much. I wrote; journaling and poetry were great healing tools. During my lowest moments, when humans couldn't comfort me, I was supported by God and the angels. I remember at this time, asking Archangel Michael to come and live with us, and he's still here with us bestowing his powerful, protective and ever loving energy upon us when needed. I guess I missed that energy only a father can give. Although I was hurting, I was blessed to have loving spirits with me.

Four years after my dad passed away, my husband died suddenly. 'Shock' doesn't even go near the place I was thrown into.

I can't even explain in words how I got through this period in my life. I was grieving for myself, and also for my two little girls who lost their dad. But we got through the difficult grieving process with the help of so many human angels, as well as our ever-present loving angels and God.

I was beginning to understand about 'soul purpose' and it was at this time I became more aware of challenges and their purpose.

I understood that some we bring to ourselves, through our thoughts or action, but others are what our soul needed to experience for our personal and spiritual growth.

Parenting alone brought so many obvious challenges, but I saw them as opportunities to grow more in trust of spirit as well as a human being. I trusted my guides and they carried me through. I dug deep and found the gifts of courage and strength and began to realise how capable and powerful I was.

**I see life so differently now.
I trust that all is well and happening
perfectly for my soul's experience.
I have been given insights and gifts
that have lit up my life
and I'm forever grateful
for being blessed with such graces.**

**My mother died three years ago,
and in total contrast
to my previous experiences
of losing a loved one, it was beautiful.**

It was her time; her soul had experienced all it needed to in her body and so, lovingly and peacefully, it lit up her path and guided her back to merge with the all-loving light source that is creation, from where she first came.

Whilst coming to terms with the loss of my mom from my physical world, I did some art therapy. Together with writing, I would often do this to help work through emotions at various times. Using colours, I would just go into my emotions and paint. Nothing in particular, just the act of putting colours together on paper unconsciously and going with the flow. I was never able to draw and only used this practice as part of my colour healing therapy. However, when my mom passed and I took to the paints, I started to create pictures; real pictures! A gift left to me,

I believe, through my mom's loving energy light as she passed.

As I shared with others more and more of my spiritual awakening and the wisdom and insights given to me, it seemed more and more people were opening themselves up to another way of looking at life and its challenges and were asking my thoughts on certain matters.

From my experience and work with children, I offer advice and support to parents who seek it. I believe parenting has become more difficult in recent times, and indeed childhood is not as it was. The innocence of childhood leaves them far earlier nowadays and I believe there is guidance needed for parents who endeavour to raise emotionally healthy young adults. I am there, locally, to offer advice and support for parents who ask.

I also offer support and advice to people seeking spiritual guidance; helping them make sense of their life situations. I find that those who have suffered, or suffering serious health conditions, come to me for guidance and comfort.

I offer this part of myself to people as 'service'. I believe the helping of others, where we give ourselves through the energy of love, is the most important gift we can give along our life's path. Giving ourselves, without reward, is what I personally believe to be what future generations will do.

I imagine a future world without money, where people, with all their different and diverse gifts, will share those gifts with each other and in this way, all needs of all people would be met and we will share a world of peace.

I am a colour therapist, sharing the colourful, powerful yet gentle energy with others. Working with the healing light of the sun, one can bring harmony, balance and change within the body and into one's life. Sunlight is broken down into the visible spectrum of coloured light, which we refer to as rainbow colours. Each colour of light carries a different vibration and influences the spiritual, emotional and physical well-being of the body, through the body's own energy centres, chakras.

Once people become aware of and understand each colour and its effects, both negatively and positively, on the body and environment, they can continue consciously to use the energy of colour to improve all levels of their being.

Colour therapy healing also includes chakra energy clearing and balancing, which is a beautiful, non-invasive, gentle healing. Once a chakra balance is completed, the client is guided to self-care and given advice on how to keep their energy centres healthy into the future. This gives people power over their own health.

Meditation, colour visualisation, crystal energy healing, and angel card readings can all or separately be included in a colour therapy/chakra balancing session. I also send distance healing where needed. Whatever I learn, as long as it benefits a person's personal or spiritual growth, I share what I believe to be true.

I am guided continually by the light. For more than 20 years I have been open to the wisdom and gifts given to me by the Creator. Through the light, I have received wisdom and knowledge through many avenues. Angels are an ongoing part of my life and I call on them for small tasks as well as bigger ones. I guess they are like an unseen family in our home. I have learned to 'be'; going with the flow and trusting I am being taken care of by spirit; the all-loving, all-knowing, powerful, forgiving, and gentle Creator: the All-That-Is. My journey continues and I am sure I have more to learn.

I have gone within, dug deep and peeled back layers of my ignorance about life, and myself, one by one. I have faced my shadow side, accepted its ugliness and transformed its darkness into light.

I have no doubt there are more layers to uncover until my soul has experienced all it desired from the moment I came into this lifetime.

When I look back over my life, I recognise points even in my childhood that seem to be linked to experiences during my adult life, and I believe at certain times, I was nudged so to speak, by spirit, to wake up to something more than my ordinary day to day life.

As a child, I sleep-walked up to the age of 18 years. It never bothered me and I thought it just a bit quirky. My mom, who always was the one that found me roaming around the house at night, never indicated to me that it was a problem. She used to say that 'some children do'. But what I think was pretty amazing when I look back now, is that each time she found me she would ask what I was doing and I would always, on every occasion, reply 'looking for the key'. Maybe that was my unconscious self, seeking the key to unlock the secrets of my soul.

When I stopped sleep-walking at 18, it was around that time that I became fascinated with all things mystical, so maybe I found my key.

I also had recurring dreams when I was about 10 or 11 years old. I would be gliding down a hallway towards a closed door. Across the door was a giant eye with the number one over it. These dreams frightened me while they lasted. Coming forward, one of the first books I read on ancient Egypt, I chose it purely for the cover, as it was a picture of a giant eye which threw me immediately back to those dreams of childhood. That book was 'The Hermetica – The Lost Wisdom of the Pharaohs'. Coincidence or something deeper, I do not know.

Times were very different 25 years ago, in rural Ireland. A country steeped in Catholicism and the churches rules, people wouldn't even entertain listening to anything outside of their own belief. Even today there are still many people who, through their fear of the unknown or maybe even religious conditioning, are reluctant to listen. Even members of my own family might call me 'weird'. But there is a younger generation coming forward in Ireland with many spiritual healing gifts and slowly but surely times are changing.

That is why I tend to let people come to me for guidance rather than push myself out there in front of them. I respect everyone's journey and if I am not to be part of their journey that is perfect. We are all at different stages of waking up to our light work and spiritual journey.

I am an empath and I find this can be difficult at times. I cannot attend funerals without feeling physically sick and weighed down with the darkness of grief. I try not to watch the news or read newspapers, as there is too much hate and sadness being reported, it upsets me greatly.

In contrast, when talking with friends about their hurts and problems, being an empath is beneficial, as I can feel the depth of their pain and intuitively know how deep it goes which helps in the type of guidance I give.

My philosophy is that we should keep our thoughts positive and loving.

What we think, say and do becomes who we are. When we keep our thoughts loving, everything else will follow.

Although brought up a Catholic, I no longer practice. I have no problem with religion and have some interest in all of them. I understand and accept that everyone has their own path. There are many roads and they all lead to the light. If I had a religion and it had a name, it would be love and peace.

I believe that I agreed to this journey before I was born. I chose my family and the life conditions which would take me through the experiences I have had, to enable me to grow in spirit and light, so that I could inspire and help others to heal and seek their own spiritual path.

I always felt compelled to share what I believed to be true, even when I knew I could be ridiculed.

**By sharing my knowledge,
I have inspired others to
find their light and undertake
their own journeys.**

The all loving Creator, like a spiritual sunrise, is beginning to flood light across the whole of our beautiful planet. Never before in history have so many Lightworkers been incarnated in the same lifetime. And never before have so many Lightworkers been needed. Our spirits, or souls, have been preparing for this time for lifetimes.

To encourage others who may be setting out on their path, I would say: Trust in your journey; be still, go within; meditate, pray; asking for guidance and one day the light within you, your soul, will spark and ignite, revealing your gifts, so you may start your journey of light work, inspiring others, helping to raise the vibration of our beautiful earth. Together, we can accomplish miracles.

(I like this quote because although it's light-hearted, it's also very wise).

'If you think you are too small to make a difference,
try sleeping with a mosquito ... '

His Holiness the 14th Dalai Lama

Always, in love and light, Ann x

Ann Hannon Hughes
I was born in Birmingham, England to Irish parents.

Always a seeker of truth and justice, it is no accident I pursued a career in Family Law, working mainly with marital breakdown and domestic violence.

After a 15 year career in Birmingham, my husband and I, as newlyweds, moved to rural Ireland, the country of our roots, to start and raise a family.

My love of children and particularly children with special needs led me to study and qualify in special needs education and I worked in my local school as a Special Needs Assistant. Having always had a passion for alternative healing, holistic therapies and all things spiritual, in recent years I studied and qualified as a Colour Healing Therapist.

I offer support and advice to those seeking personal and spiritual growth, through varied alternative methods.

Ann's Facebook page:
www.facebook.com/change.your.colour.andhealyourlife/

Trials and Tribulations

By Vanessa Kum Jew

Each Lightworker's mission is unique all with the greater purpose of personal soul growth and to assist healing of Mother Earth. It is something which is felt, something which is ingrained in them. It is who they are and why they are here physically on this earth.

I, as a Lightworker have to be the light in my own life as well as others and that is often hard. We must be a beacon for others to learn from, to be a support and to teach through the way we live our life. It is through my written voice, my spoken voice and actions that I help facilitate change in this world and hold a space for healing. We are so busy giving we often forget ourselves, we equally need to receive.

Wow what can I say, spiritual awakening is an eye opener. As it comes it can bring with it The Dark Night Of The Soul as it did with me. It tears you apart, elevates your fears bringing them to the surface, highlights your weakness's, preys on your core wounds, but on the other side is something beautiful words cannot explain. This Dark Night I have experienced three times now.

The first time I was filled with dread, felt very alone and couldn't see anything promising in the present or future.

As I was unable to sleep things were more pronounced. I wasn't emotionally coping, I wanted to reach out to someone but who, who would understand, who could help. Unbeknown to me at the time I was releasing.

My next Dark Night came two years later. This one was very different and like last time came out of nowhere.

A sudden overwhelming feeling that everything was falling apart for no apparent reason but my mind made sure there were plenty of reasons.

This period was longer this time, about a month. I isolated myself from everyone thinking quiet would be my saviour, bringing answers. It was at this time I found EFT, or tapping. I struggled with it, not giving it a chance, not being able to stay focused long enough to spend enough time with it. This was my answer yet I couldn't see it as I was self sabotaging. The third Dark Night came just 3 months later, with a vengeance. I had constant anxiety, many severe panic attacks, I couldn't drive, my perception had gone. I hardly slept and called in all my healer friends for help.

My family didn't understand what I was going through, there was nothing wrong in the outside world, why I couldn't function doing things I would normally do. The one constant I kept was posting the daily star signs on my Facebook page sometimes taking so much longer to write than usual. How did I come out of these Dark Nights, it was just time that made it easier, trying as best I could to eat good food, when I could eat, limit or reduce coffee and rest as much as possible.

Since my awakening my sensitivity has heightened greatly.

Having always been an empath, my senses are far more tuned in to the environment. I can't watch the news I have to listen to it, I feel vibration and frequency quite easily and it can be disruptive to my own energy. As I am a very visual person. I can desensitise to a degree, but it is harder having viewed something which is of a harsh nature, something I have to be very conscious of. I am concerned with what I put in and on my body and when a change comes it literally happens overnight. I have made my own natural hair dyes, toothpaste, shampoo, moisturiser, I don't drink tap water or wear nail polish. I am more concerned now with the affect on the environment now with what I use, what I do in the day to day. So to understand how I got to the day of my first awakening we have to go back to the beginning.

As a child I always had an interest and curiosity in witchcraft, Salem, Haiti, psychic abilities, telepathy and Tarot cards. I would be drawn to books, television shows with a connection to anything a little different in nature or the supernatural.

It wasn't until later in adult life where things came to light for me and began to fall into place like a puzzle. I thoughts these were just interests, me being curious about the unknown but they are in fact me.

My marriage came to an end and I turned to something to help me get through, give me strength, direction. I would go to New Age stores looking for books, if I brought one home

I was happy. It was like a safety blanket. I read with varied interests until I came to a point where I stopped purchasing books and found strength in knowing I no longer needed them, relied on them. I turned to crystals, more so for my children as pretty stones. It was through Facebook I found some support or help if you like. Spiritual pages jumped out at me, I had liked so many but they each gave me something. I would put my name down on many reading threads regularly hoping someone would help me, lead me. Rarely did I receive a reading, why I would think, I need one.

It wasn't till years later I realised I didn't receive one because I needed to work things out on my own, to realise I didn't need someone to tell me what to do. It was at this time someone walked into my life propelling me forward at a fast pace changing my life forever.

They were my greatest teacher and one of my hardest lessons and for that I am forever grateful. They took me to where I needed to be spiritually and personally and pushed me to reawaken and remember so much deeply held wisdom for they held the key.

This is where past lives really opened up for me. You see we had already travelled so many lives together, all of which were out of balance and karmically challenged. And now, as things stand, I do feel we still have more lives to work through together but now I feel equipped to do so.

It was through this relationship I was introduced to mirroring and had to face some confronting things about myself. I also discovered two people could have the same core wounds yet display them completely different. This relationship was karmic, a false twin flame and they were a narcissist. A triple whammy and I wouldn't wish for things to have been any different.

My memories came through as life called for them, as inner knowledge, I could pluck as I needed it.

The memories forced me to feel, to understand, to think, to theorise and to come to my own conclusions rather than accept what is said and written.

I became very aware of energy, especially the energetic connection between people and the depth and the source of it. With this also came the understanding of disconnection with self and others. Energy can be both destructive and healing depending on the emotions that charge it. It was here I learnt to detach, well as much as possible. I was here for the lessons but with emotional distance. My hand was also forced to understand The Law of Attraction. I was living it, as we all are, so in order to grow I had to follow it's Laws.

It took time but I learnt how to love unconditionally, to be vulnerable, holding back versus giving, lower energies, energetic cords and cord cutting, acceptance of others and situations as well as self acceptance, personal empowerment and so much about the soul and specifically my soul.

I discovered I was a fixer and drew in people and situations that I thought I could fix but really, I had to mend the broken parts of me. It is only through the power of love you can lead someone to their own light and tear down those walls.

This relationship showed I had been allowing myself to be controlled and dictated by others throughout my life. I had not set sufficient boundaries nor was I strong enough to uphold them. I had not learnt to support myself and back myself at every turn. What really spoke to me was the fact that over the four and a half years together I never smiled or laughed once within this relationship. Another wounded one cannot fill the void, only you can fill that yourself with love.

I learnt to stand up for myself and found my self respect. I had to learn truth, authenticity and to take off my protective mask.

Our time together was much a journey of self. Sometimes you just have to know when something is done and you have to walk away for your highest good. Sometimes that is your lesson. It was also during this time when something occurred that I still can't really explain. It was when an aquaintance and I crossed paths and we chatted all things spiritual not knowing this was each of our world. A few hours passed like only a few moments and we parted. By time I got home I had a headache and really dry mouth. I knew it had to do with the two of us meeting. I was tempted to call and say what I was experiencing but decided to leave it. A few days later we had that conversation, both had experienced the same symptoms and wanted to call.

We both felt the connection, he felt it was past life, I don't feel that, perhaps a new connection. A significant moment for both of us.

The turning point where all the accumulated learned knowledge came together was when I literally woke up one morning and said with confidence 'today I'm going to give a reading' and did.

I never looked back and that was where it all began. My life had changed forever. I found what made my heart sing.

Acceptance was tough and only came out to my family and friends in the last two years. When it came to sharing with my mum I only told her inadvertently, I had given up my job to work full time with what I love. I had no choice but to explain how I was going to support my family and I really only told her the basics and she didn't really ask any questions. This is not her world. Whenever the subject comes up she replies with something like 'you've always been into that weird stuff.'

I have found acceptance with who I am and understanding that my mum will never understand me or what I do and she probably doesn't accept it and that's ok. We are on different paths.

When I left my job I followed the calling to take a leap of faith. It took me two months to trust enough to leave and pursue what I love, all that I am and all that I was to become. It wasn't too long after I realised the leap of faith wasn't referring to my business but it was my time to heal, learn tough lessons and grow. Leaving my job created the time and the space for me to do so. I had many light bulb moments, times of being stuck, confused and so many tears. It took me some time to really feel ready to step into who I am and feel worthy enough and capable of being that person. I struggled with the religious/spiritual factor. I am a Catholic, a non practising one. In some way I felt as though I was betraying the religion, God, the faith I had grown up with. I had to work out how to bring the two together and be comfortable with it. I had to let it come to me rather than think about it, rationalise it.

The angels I would call in for assistance are actually God's helpers and when I call upon any Higher Beings or The Divine it is God. In the end there is no betrayal of my religion but rather a beautiful union of love.

Over the years as I have grown personally so has my direction. I started off doing card readings, then intuitive before I found healing which is where my heart lies.

I have studied many areas of the metaphysical while at the same time remembered from my accumulation of lives. I consider myself an energy alchemist where I take energy and transform it making it my own.

I like to come to my own conclusions about things, trusting how the answers feel within my body.

I work with many energies on a daily basis. I am a Reiki Master Teacher, Crystal Therapist, Flower Therapist, Intuitive and Angel/Oracle card Reader. I see past lives, write and facilitate meditation, an inspirationalist, a motivator, space clearer, I write courses, blogs and the daily star signs and I love working with children as they are our future, our tomorrow. Animal Totems/Spirit Guides offer us invaluable information about where we are at, what we must do and where we need help. They are nature, they are also us. When you understand your animal guide you understand yourself. Flowers are powerful healers, the messages they bring, their beauty, their diversity and their place in the natural world have something to offer which is a unique gift. Working with their energies, fragrance and the memories they invoke bring forth immense healing.

Past lives have become a real passion, an eye opener and something that has really opened up a new side of me. Past lives explain so much, give you a deeper understanding of who you are and why. While I read a lot, I found I just knew things, remembered and felt how things work and come together across all planes, dimensions and timelines.

My mission statement is this, to create the physical world we desire we must be the person we are, no more no less. It starts with ourselves then as a collective we become one with who we are and the place in which we live.

I am here to assist those who are ready to walk their spiritual path and step into who they truly are and to support those that aren't, so together we can bring healing to ourselves and the earth. I have two mottos: 'Stop thinking, start feeling'.

Everyone gets caught up in their head, if they felt whether something is right for them rather than thinking they would be able to trust themselves a lot more, find solutions, answers and understand themselves. The other is 'The answer is always simple'. Often the most simple answer is the one yet we continue to look believing it to be incorrect, too easy.

This work is so rewarding, to help someone to understand, to be able to guide another through difficulties and to facilitate someone's healing is truly satisfying and amazing. My advice to anyone taking this journey, embrace who you are and never fear it or reject it. The blessings and joy it will bring you cannot be surpassed.

Be yourself, be open, face your fears, be vulnerable.
We are all Lightworkers, some have found their feet,
some are not aware. Either way live with integrity
and flow within life within it's ebbs and flows.
Some days are more of a challenge than others,
don't resist, accept the challenge with grace.

Namaste Vanessa Kum Jew

Vanessa Kum Jew

Vanessa is your healer able to bring about life changes, clarity and acceptance while guiding you to personal empowerment.

As an energetic weaver she is able to bring unhealed emotions to the surface enabling you to open your awareness, find perspective and widen your perception.

A Reiki Master, Crystal Therapist, psychic intuitive, past life visionary mentor, writer, meditation facilitator, Flower Therapist, Space Clearer, she has a spiritual tool bag of gifts to offer you through her business The Essence Within.

Vanessa is passionate about her work promoting positivity and encouragement at every step. Vanessa's life purpose and mission is to offer a compassionate and committed approach to your needs enabling you to return to the natural state of the authentic, limitless self.

To connect with Vanessa on Facebook
www.facebook.com/theessencewithin

Website:
The Spiritual Alchemist
www.theessencewithin.wixsite.com/
spiritual-alchemist

The Rainbow Journey of an
Ascending Seedling

By Jo Nicholls

When I agreed to enter this lifetime, I thought it would be a good idea to jam-pack it full of challenges, obstacles, lessons and other such opportunities for growth. This understanding has been key to my personal growth, my attitude to life and it shades the undertones of my sense of humour.

Early on Sunday morning, the 24th of October 1982, my naked screaming self arrived here on Earth, ready to start another round of what us humans call Life. While the energy of a balanced Libra intrigued me, I had already used my gift of stubborn determination to hold out and arrive a week late, under the Scorpio sun and here began a lifetime of personal development, a journey of growth and change more powerful than a butterfly's, which has made me the true spiritual warrior I am today.

In my life so far, I have learnt that everything which challenges us can be a lesson and that everything can be accepted or overcome, given time, support and the right frame of mind. My lessons have certainly been challenging, right from the start of this life. I learnt from a young age that caregivers can fail to care, and worse, that children can be in danger from those they should be able to trust.

> **As a child I learnt to hide,**
> **my throat closing,**
> **heart pounding and mind racing,**
> **wrestling with fear, pain and guilt.**
> **I learnt that just when you think**
> **you've escaped from a monster's lair,**
> **you can run right into another lair,**
> **another prison.**
> **And this, this is one of many**
> **experiences I have learned to overcome.**

The courage embedded in my soul enabled me to accept and learn important lessons from my childhood and early adulthood. It enabled me to use my experiences as tools for growth. I know that a seed can germinate in the absence of light, that its leaves naturally grow towards the light. In the same way, my seed of courage grew into a tree that has stretched its leaves above the canopy and into the light.

> **Life has taught me a lot about**
> **light and darkness. It has taught me**
> **that we are all made of both light and dark.**

If we try to lock our darkness up, to shut it away in a closet like a skeleton, to stamp on it or to smudge it away, to cover it with expensive oils, we fail to learn from it and we lose a valuable part of ourselves.

Carl Jung taught us that we don't become enlightened by imagining figures of light, but by making the darkness conscious.

Consequently, enlightenment is not about shutting the door against the darkness, but about exploring what's behind the door, safe in the knowledge that there is not just light and dark in us, but a whole rainbow of colours. Working in the light is not about being perfect, but about knowing ourselves and our flaws and knowing and accepting ourselves as perfectly flawed individuals.

Knowing myself and understanding the world around me has been a very important part of my spiritual journey and personal development has played a key role in this. Because I learnt to be self-reliant from a young age, I learnt how to achieve goals through effort and determination. I have attained a brown belt in karate, have won rosettes in horse riding gymkhanas and have successfully bred prize-winning dogs, amongst other things. My goal at that time was simply to achieve the best results I could, in whichever field interested me. One of my fields of interest was in understanding how the mind and emotions work.

Studying counselling and psychology led me to the understand an important lesson about goals – that often the most important personal goals are the ones you do not receive a certificate for.

Knowing that my children would learn from the example I set, I realised the importance of achieving the goal of loving and nurturing myself. I have enjoyed watching my children grow, seeing them thrive like saplings in rich soil, in a positive and encouraging environment.

As part of this lifetime's journey, I have explored and studied many spiritual practices. This is because, like a bee flitting from flower to flower, my brain flits quickly from one subject to another. I have learnt to accept my ADHD, not as a limitation, but as a superpower! Although my brain rapidly moves from one topic to the next, it never loses sight of the big picture – like the bee I am learning about the garden as a whole and about the forest beyond. For some people, my rapid thought processes can seem overwhelming, but I manage to keep sight of the bigger picture and in this picture, many different spiritual practices have their place.

Through my spiritual exploration, I have learnt that self-mastery requires combining the physical, emotional, mental and spiritual aspects of ourselves.

In order to develop physically, I have practiced yoga and am a naturopath dietician and herbalist. I have studied and used counselling and life-coaching to increase my knowledge and awareness of our emotions, our thought processes and triggers. Having studied Child Social and Emotional Development, I have learnt the importance of nurturing children on their spiritual path, rather than shutting them down due to conservatism and conformity. I am trained to provide support to breast-feeding mothers and in my work/volunteering I dip into several modalities of healing– holistic therapies, massage, sound and colour therapies, aromatherapy and crystal therapies. I have found that healing involves more than one approach and that a holistic approach best suits our complex human natures.

What my varied experiences have taught me above all, however, is relatively simple. Ultimately, we are energy and when we understand this we become more aware of our purpose. We are on Earth to grow and to do so we need to travel our own paths, as best we can. I don't see it as my job to fix people nor to push my beliefs onto other people. I am here to continue my own journey and to support others into becoming aware. Being kind to others and respecting their journey is important. So, I continue my journey, helping others when invited to, by encouraging awareness of ourselves and awareness of ourselves as energy.

On my own journey of personal and spiritual growth, I have met many interesting and inspiring people. I have friends who are shamans, Christians, Buddhists, pagans and witches. I have sat in a circle and explored mediumship, as well as practicing aspects of holistic therapies and I work with meridians and chakras.

For me, there is little need to draw lines between these different practices – for me, it comes down to working with energy.

> **I do not feel the need to label myself
> or the methods I use when healing.
> I am who I am,
> a soul on a journey,
> and I believe there are many ways
> of being in touch with spirit.**

One of the main reasons I dislike labels, is because they are limiting. To some people labels are important, providing a kind of order in a chaotic world and giving people the illusion of control.

> **Labelling people, however,
> means putting them into boxes
> and our true energy cannot
> be contained in this way.**

> **I am often asked if I am a witch,
> or a Lightworker, a pagan or a healer.
> But what do these labels really mean?**

A witch is someone who lives, breathes and communicates with nature, someone who understands the power of energy, the invisible power that enables the moon to draw the tides.

A Lightworker is someone who makes a choice to continually raise their own vibration and to share this higher vibration with others.

According to these definitions I am both a witch and a Lightworker, but I am so much more – I am energy, spirit and for me, this does not need a label.

In my late twenties, I retired from work, due to a progressive health condition. Living with a physical disability remains challenging in many ways, but my Scorpio stubbornness has kept me out of a wheelchair and kept me as active as I can be. Libra is dominant in my birth chart, however, and perhaps explains why I see so much beauty in nature. My garden is my sacred space and it is full of life and colour. Friends have helped me in its creation, by gifting plants and helping with bigger jobs that I would be unable to achieve alone and in doing so, their energy has helped to create this special place. My physical limits mean I don't travel far and wide, but I don't need to – stepping out into my garden is like stepping into an oasis – friends have commented that just sitting in my garden is a healing experience. Its ever-changing beauty is a project that keeps me active, in touch with nature and which brings me joy.

Rather than dwelling on what I lost, when I had to give up my career, I focused on the doors that this opened for me. The time I had for personal development grew, as did the time and energy I had to help and support other people in their journeys. I do have to be aware of my fluctuating energy levels; because of this I balance rest and activity, helping others and looking after myself, but I generally get this balance right – and I probably have my balanced Libra energy to thank for this.

In recent years, one of the most important lessons I have learnt is that if you want to change the world, you need to begin with yourself. When you focus on yourself, you grow and the universe supports this.

Being authentic and having no agenda other than a journey of personal growth – this helps us ascend. Focusing too much on other people's paths can cause us to take our eye off the ball and we find that the plates we've been so carefully spinning fall to the floor.

> **Spiritual growth is not**
> **even and predictable.**
> **Ego is a common barrier to growth**
> **that we all have to battle with.**

> **We may aim to raise our vibration,**
> **to increase the light that's inside us,**
> **but as soon as we perceive**
> **ourselves to be a shining light,**
> **setting an example for others,**
> **we have fallen into ego's trap.**

We find that instead of being a shining light, we have stumbled into the shadows. Everyone on a spiritual path faces this challenge and that's why self-awareness and knowledge of self is such an important part of the spiritual journey. We may learn to use the many tools at our disposal – whether tarot cards, rituals, crystals or meditation – but if we don't learn who we are first, ego can easily waylay us.

> **In order to avoid ego-led thoughts**
> **and behaviour, I believe that we need to**
> **know ourselves, to be mindful and aware.**

If we are accountable for our actions and take responsibility for the choices we make, we are better able to see life from the perspective of ourselves as souls. I see this as being 'awake' – we begin to recognise that we are spiritual beings on a path of discovery.

In supporting other people on their paths, I learned to draw on both my counselling skills and on a range of healing practices. Once on this path, happily volunteering my time and energy, I soon realised that I needed a special space, a place which would become part of a healing experience for visitors and which would also be a sanctuary where I could recharge and maintain my own energy levels.

I began to visualise what is now the Crystal Sanctuary, a deceptively small wooden cabin at the end of my holistic medicine garden. Using the practice of manifestation I worked hard to achieve what I had visualised.

My cabin is now such an amazing space – an abundance of crystals combine to create its unique energy; there are also visual representations of angels, unicorns and goddesses supporting the positive energy. People have told me that the Crystal Sanctuary heals and empowers. A friend came to visit me a while after her partner had died in a plane crash. She arrived feeling broken, in despair and unable to shake the panic which had gripped her since learning of her partner's death. We sat and talked.

After a short time she told me that spending time with me in the sanctuary had eased the shock and dread, that for the first time in weeks, she was able to feel a sense of peace.

This is how the Crystal Sanctuary helps people; there are healing crystals which vibrate in its very foundations.

Of course, each individual that I am able to support represents an important achievement – one that doesn't need a certificate – and I am often fortunate to be supported by people in return, whether emotionally, spiritually, or by them dropping by because I have been quiet for a while or to help me with jobs in my garden.

When a range of different people in my life began to suggest that I open a spiritual centre, in order to provide a place where both myself and others could reach out to and to support more people, I declined, aware that creating my own centre would be a lot of additional work and of the risk of acting on or developing ego.

> **It took several years and quite a few more refusals before I was urged to recognise the message for what it was – the universe was giving me a nudge.**

Knowing my physical limitations and wanting to steer clear of ego traps, I agreed to facilitate the process of starting up a spiritual centre, which has now come into existence and been welcomed by the local community.

From the outset the ethos of the Lighthouse Spiritual Wellbeing Community Centre has been that it is run collectively, by the community and for the community. In its creation, I was fortunate to be able to bring people together from many different backgrounds, so that together we could pool our skills, our knowledge and our experience to create a spiritual centre which is not owned or led by any one person – at its core, the Lighthouse is there to be a place of relaxation, laughter, light and hope, where both volunteers and visitors can be supported in their unique spiritual journeys without judgement or agenda.

The Lighthouse is a centre for learning. The emphasis on learning is important. Learning is key to our growth – by learning who we truly are, we can learn to grow beyond the confines of our previous expectations. When we know ourselves fully, when we recognise ourselves as energy, as souls, we begin to see with Crystal Clear Vision, a concept I developed when supporting people in the Crystal Sanctuary.

**So much of life is about learning
and sharing what we have learnt
in order to improve each other's lives.**

It is about both accepting help and giving support. Together we can raise our awareness, our vibrations and in turn we can help others to do the same, if that is what is asked of us.

The human experience is what I believe we are all here to learn from, even if that is to simply live through it. It is beautifully imperfect, simply complex, easily impossible and an effortless challenge. Living through the human experience takes us on a rollercoaster ride of joy and despair and everything in between. Our world is constantly changing and we can easily get lost in its familiarity. We need to remember that we are souls, bright, beautiful and rainbow-hued. We are energy vibrating at many frequencies and we are learning and growing and that is a wonderful thing. When we shed our perception of the human experience as being all that there is, we can emerge from our chrysalis, spread our wings and truly fly; in doing so we allow our inner light to shine.

Jo Nicholls

Jo lives in Essex in the UK. She studied child psychology and counselling as part of her own healing journey and proceeded to use these skills that came naturally to her in helping others too.

Passionate about self awareness being the foundation to spiritual growth, and driven by her own experiences she began looking into, studying, and incorporating into her daily life a variety of holistic approaches to wellbeing. With encouragement from friends and neighbours, Jo started sharing her experiences, tips, knowledge and energy with others through her Facebook page, The Crystal Sanctuary – the home of Crystal Clear Vision, in her free time.

Grateful for an amazing group of friends, and the ability to maintain a healthy spiritual, mental and emotional state regardless of physical limitations, Jo makes sure that others have a place to feel safe, supported, understood, empowered and encouraged, preventing a state of overwhelm.

Find out more here:
www.TheCrystalSanctuary.webs.com
www.Facebook.com/Crystal.Sanctuary

Touched by Love
One Lightworker's Journey Home

By Sharon Miralles

As a small child I knew I was different, I could sense energy which at times frightened me. With my extremely sensitive nature, I preferred to be in solitude than with the company of other children. They didn't understand me. Even my own mother, as loving as she was, didn't understand me or my sensitivities. As I told her of my experiences and memories of before I was born and of my past lives, which I had in my waking consciousness, she laughed and said 'that is not possible'. My memories and visions were real – very real to me.

Ever since I can remember, I knew I was more than just my body. I was aware of my consciousness; I could feel my soul and I had a hard time accepting that I was in a body. How strange it felt. I remember sitting in our garden amongst the trees, staring up at the sunny sky with my hands touching my face, feeling every curve and thinking this isn't me.

I did accept it, but continued in my solitude, preferring my own company than those of other people and children, who at times were cruel. My sensitive nature drove me further and further inside myself as I saw the harsh realities of the World.

Growing up I endured the mental and emotional abuse of my alcoholic father. I witnessed my mother, who I loved dearly, suffer at his hands. My childhood was no fun.

I grew deeper and deeper into a depressed state. This had been something I struggled with my whole life, until later years when I found ways to cope and heal through the practice of Reiki which has been such a blessing.

In addition to my painful childhood, haunted by unhappy memories, I suffered more painful relationships and two miscarriages. I had two beautiful children whom I adored, but suffering severe post natal depression and grieving the loss of my beloved mother, I found myself spiralling into the depths of total despair.

I felt like I was in a dark hole and I couldn't get out. I hardly recognise the person I once was now when I look back on my life. It feels strange to talk about those days because I know that I am healed.

I can honestly say that through all of my adversities and hardships in life, I am stronger and a better person. I can reach out to others with empathy, love and compassion and inspire others to heal. I share that part of my life with you, so you can know, believe or at least have hope that you too can heal and not be defined by your past or your life circumstances. I am healed, whole and aligned with my Divine soul. I am a Lightworker here to heal the World and spread my light!

Through my journey of self healing and self discovery I did not see this. I had to find my light within. I dismissed all the signs from Heaven trying to reach out to me.

One night I was awakened during the night by an Angel standing at the bottom of my bed.

So large, illuminated in bright, white light and I was immediately comforted. I rubbed my eyes in awe at the majestic presence that stood at my feet. This profound and beautiful experience stayed with me. As I shared my experience, there were some people in my life who did not believe me. I stopped talking about the beautiful Angel who appeared to me.

Vivid dreams, visitations from my mother and Angel appearances continued. I had dreams repeatedly of the word 'Reiki'. I did not even know what this was. I did not listen. I eventually blocked all of my spiritual experiences and delved further into religion. I found great comfort and a friendship with God during this time. I began a journey of self discovery and realisation.

I began to heal myself from the past and learn to love myself, a concept which was so unfamiliar to me. To love and accept oneself is the most difficult lesson in life most people struggle with.

Growing up with so much self-hatred and abuse, this was a monumental undertaking indeed! I spent much time in contemplative reflection and in communion and conversation with God. I began to feel my Divine soul once more, like I did when I was a child. I felt myself expand and fill with love.

I felt alive, awakened and as though a veil had been lifted. As such a surprise to me I began an unexpected healing journey.

After my second caesarean and subsequent surgery to remove scar tissue, I had severe pain. I remember one night praying as I always did before going to sleep and asking God to heal my discomfort and pain. I very naturally placed my hands over my caesarean scar and was totally surprised and amazed to feel a tingling, warm sensation in my hands and in my body under my hands. It felt comforting and soothing.

I did this every night for three months and the pain disappeared. There had been times I could hardly walk with the pain and now it was gone!

I absolutely knew without a doubt that there was something going on with my hands as one night I placed my hands upon my dying cat who laid listlessly on the lounge. After twenty minutes of intense heat, she got up and walked like there was nothing wrong with her! She came to me for healing every day (and she gave me a healing also) and she lived another seven years.

I finally learnt Reiki, but I do it my way, which is very natural to me. The Angels began appearing to me again as well as Ascended Master Jesus, Mother Mary and other Light Beings with their loving messages and guidance.

I now help others to heal and to remember their soul and true spiritual nature which is pure love and light – energy.

I connect with their soul, see their soul colour and energy vibration and know just what they need in order to fulfil their Divine life purpose.

With the help of the Angels and Ascended Masters and with my past life visions I now help other people clear out their own painful memories which are holding them back from fulfilling their own Divine life purpose.

I love when I touch people and they know they have experienced the Divine. I love when I see the shift in them and their light is re-awakened and they connect once more with their soul.

This is my purpose; to raise the vibrations of others and collectively raise the vibrations of the world; to awaken the Christ Consciousness or Unity Consciousness. This is my gift to humanity and the World.

Through all those I come into contact with, through my healing practice and writing work and by spreading Divine messages, if I touch a heart and soul in some small way, then I have succeeded in spreading more light in this World. This gives me great joy.

My other greatest joy and my purpose for Being is my children. My children are the greatest teachers, healers and comfort to me. They are the love of my life. They inspire me to live each day.

I know they were put on this Earth to help me to heal and to heal others. They too are Lightworkers here to make a difference in this World. They have helped me in ways too numerous and immense to express. I believe and understand all of their experiences and sensitivities. With all my heart I live for them.

This was all confirmed to me through a near death experience. An experience so profound, it changed my life forever.

I remember vividly as if it were yesterday. After all my self-discovery and self healing, my Earthy mission was over.

One night before bed I felt terribly unwell and I knew there was something seriously wrong with me. A sharp pain pieced my head, repeatedly. I felt faint and lay down.

I left my body and I floated above and then suddenly began travelling at great speed. The whole time being comforted by a familiar light and love which enveloped me. It felt beautiful. I was home; the most glorious feeling.

In one split second, I thought 'I don't want to leave my girls' and in an instance I was back inside my body. A loving Being in brilliant, white light appeared beside my bed. They explained to me that I had finished everything on Earth I had came to do. I had fulfilled my lessons and life purpose. I told them I didn't want to leave my daughters. They said to me if I stayed there would be suffering. I asked them what suffering. They repeated again that there would be suffering. I agreed and was taken to a special place with them to discuss my new purpose for this life.

First and foremost I was to be there for my daughters; guiding and nurturing them through life and helping them with their mission. Secondly, I was to help all those I come into contact with through my healing work. Thirdly, I was to help heal the World through my writing work; sharing Divine messages with the World. My life was no longer a personal mission but rather a global mission. I feel grateful and honoured to undertake this Divine mission.

The suffering I believe is the harshness and density of Earth life, I feel deeply with my sensitive Being. I honour my sensitivities as they make me who I am – a Lightworker.

The Angels help me by encouraging me to spend more time alone and just send healing and love to the planet. This is a great gift I can give to heal the planet, as by sending out love and high vibrations it raises the vibrations of the Earth and all on it. So now even when I'm alone, I can effect others in positive ways.

You can affect the World and others positively too! No matter who you are, no matter what is going on in your life: you always have a Divine light within, shining brightly. Shine, love and touch others with your light!

Every moment spent in love has positive effects. So simple yet has a ripple effect far beyond what any of us can imagine.

Your healing light is needed on this planet more than ever before. Align yourself with your light, your soul and purpose for being on this planet. Do not be afraid but take comfort in knowing that powerful Light Beings surround you; work with you and through you for the ascension of planet Earth and all those on it. You have a Divine mission through loving service on Earth and you are never alone.

Those who are ready will see your light. You will inspire, heal and support others. Do not be concerned of feeling different or what others think of you. Hold your light steady and share it with others. Be the powerful light bearer you were called to be! With love, light and unity,

Sharon Miralles

Sharon Miralles

Sharon is an intuitive healer and spiritual teacher, guided by the loving wisdom of the Creator, her Higher Self, the Angels and Ascended Masters. She is a certified Angel Intuitive, Angel Oracle Card Reader and Reiki Master Teacher.

Sharon delivers Divine messages and healings to help other souls evolve along their spiritual journey. Sharon teaches how working and connecting with loving Beings of light – such as the Archangels and Ascended Masters – can enrich our lives, creating more peace, harmony and wellbeing.

Through her first published work the 'Jesus Affirmation Cards', Sharon wishes to help re-connect people to their own Divine light, to the Creator and to the love that connects us all. By raising the collective consciousness to higher vibrations and bringing forth the Christ Consciousness – a pure vibration of love – we can live in light, love and unity.

For more information you can visit her website at:
www.lightdivinehealings.com

Raúl's Angelic
Journey

By Raúl Estévez

Dear Souls living a Human Experience, my name is Raúl Estévez. I was born in Uruguay, South America fifty three years ago (I know, last century!) to Juan Carlos and Blanca Violeta Estévez. I was the youngest of three; my siblings were two girls, Cristina and Marilyn. I am a proud Australian. This is home to me!

My journey as a Lightworker started before I was born when my soul chose my parents, as well as the family and country I would be born into. I accepted then, as I accept now, the lessons my soul needed to experience to continue evolving though LOVE.

Due to my umbilical cord being wrapped around my neck twice, my birth was via caesarean. My late mother bared the scar, and in those days a huge incision was made on her tummy in perpendicular directions.

**I was born happy and with
rosy cheeks with not much effort,
although I had fluid in my lungs
due to the doctors leaving
their intervention a bit too long!**

From a young age, I suffered from asthma. I did swimming lessons to increase my lung capacity, and by my early twenties it was gone! I did have a very happy childhood overall, although I always felt different from others. I clearly remember feeling more comfortable around girls than boys, and I was not into soccer, which disappointed my late father because he was a fanatic all his life!

My mother always prided herself in making certain we, her children, always looked our best; to the point of having tailor made clothing (little suits for me and dresses for my sisters). All of our shoes where handcrafted to measure, which is something I do not see around anymore. She would take us to 'Zapateria Veloz' (zapateria in Spanish means shoe store, veloz means rapid, speedy) and they would measure our feet before we chose our favourite style. Two weeks later, voila! Beautiful shoes!

**As much as my mother
loved us and was caring,
she was also heavy handed,
and I suffered physical abuse at her hands.**

**I have since forgiven her,
although I have not forgotten.**

Little statuesques of angels were always around us, including a picture of a guardian angel by the front door to always protect us as we went about our day (I still have one at my home now, and I look at it before leaving home).

My first encounter with the angels was when I was about eight years old when I had an accident whilst jumping over a fence.

You can read more about it in my book, 'My Angels – Connections'. Since that day, the angels never left me; always talking, to me showing me the way and providing me with guidance, which I might add, was not always followed! Nonetheless, they never left me.

My father insisted on bringing me to soccer matches, but my only interest was getting an ice cream and a hotdog and jumping up and down the steps on the stadium. Many times we left early because I was a nuisance to my dad. He even got me into a kid's team, which was a disaster. I ended up kicking for the other team, and little did we both know that this would also become a reality, when I came out as gay in my early teens.

When I came out to my parents, they both told me I was a degenerate and a pervert for liking boys.

I was only in my very early teens and apart from having very strong feelings for boys, I hadn't had any sexual experience yet! It was very hard to hear that from my parents and also, living in a country where being a homosexual in those years was illegal. Once, some friends and I were stopped in the middle of the street by two policemen who asked us if we were gay, which of course we denied. It's sad to say that in those days, a gay person being taken in and raped by the police was not considered to be the worst that could happen. Thanks to the angels, the police moved on and we were left alone to continue walking. It was a very scary experience and neither of us could get home fast enough!

> **My late grandma understood me and always reminded me that I had not changed and that I was still lovable, by her and by the angels.**

I used to talk to her and she would tell me, 'You will find a partner and when you do it will be for life.' Wayne and I have now been together for thirty years. I was very glad that Wayne got to meet her before she passed away. I used to say to Grandma that I wanted to be a citizen of the world and she would always encourage me with my dreams and aspirations. Little did I know that my middle sister Cristina would move to Australia, and a few years later she sponsored my parents and I to move here as well.

> **It was such a beautiful act of love and angelically sent. Finally, I had found home!**

I was totally immersed in the Australian way of living and refused my parent's idea of joining the Uruguayan Club in Sydney, where they found themselves comfortable. It was not for me. I was determined to love my new home and be a full part of it. I do recall one day on my way to the train station in Sydney, seeing two police officers walking towards me and I felt total fear. I could not help but cross the road. In those years in Australia, being gay was not illegal, but I was still carrying that fear and it took a little getting used to before I was able to release that fear.

One year after arriving in Australia; my mother passed away from cancer. I have never done anything more scary and confronting than to translate from the doctor to my mum that she only had six months to live. With tears in my eyes, I told her. I could not have lied because she was attentively looking into my eyes, which she knew never, ever lied. During that six-month period, I was studying hospitality management and going to the hospital to take turns between family members to take care of her. Many times she only wanted to be showered by me and not the nurses, and in moments of lucidity, she would feel ashamed that her only son was giving her a shower. I remember telling her one day, 'Mum, you gave me my life and this is the least I can do for you with love.' My mum also gifted me at the time a gold bracelet with my initials on it, because she knew she would not see me graduate. I wore that bracelet to every single one of my university graduations.

The day she passed away I was at the NSW State Library studying when the librarian called me on the loud speaker, asking me to approach the desk. My sister was on the phone and told me to rush to Westmead Hospital in Sydney, where Mum was because the doctors said Mum did not have much longer to live. I got into my orange 1973 Honda Civic and drove within the speed limit and capacity of my car as quickly as possible. All of my family was around her. She was waiting for me and told me she finally understood, and gave me her message:

'Raúl, every time you see a butterfly, it will bring a beautiful message from me to you.'

The day of my very first book launch in Melbourne, September 2016, which was held outdoors, a white butterfly flew past between the audience and myself as I was giving my speech and many said, 'Raúl, did you see it?' which I replied 'Yes.' I looked up to the sky and said 'Thank you, Mum.' I have also felt her presence during my book signing in Sydney October 2016, which was validated by a new friend Kevin who said he could see my mum hugging me from behind.

I have been very fortunate that my country, Australia, afforded me a career and a great life style. I have studied hospitality, worked in international hotels here at home and overseas – from cleaning toilets, to becoming Director of Learning and Development. I graduated from Melbourne University with a Master of Education, always guided by my angels. My first employer as a teacher paid for my Diploma in Teaching at Melbourne University and then I financed all of the other degrees myself. Talk about angelic synchronicity; the symbol of Melbourne University is an angel in flight! Thank you, angels for always guiding me! Although, I must say, that reconciling my spiritual belief in angels and the Creator were challenged by the academic world and their constant need for empirical evidence, even though the symbol of the university is still an angel.

> **People asked me at the time
> what did I did for a living
> and my answer was always,
> 'I help people learn.'**

My dream was to travel the world as an educator and colleagues and friends used to say to me, 'Oh Raúl, teachers don't travel.' Little did they know, that in 1996 I was asked to be a part of a team of teachers going to Malaysia to help train new employees from a brand new five star hotel!

The first trip set the scene for me as an international educator. I travelled the world over more than eight times, helping people learn (in so many countries) and learning so much myself. I have been very fortunate to visit places that to some people, are just a dream, although that reality came at price. I was always away from Wayne, my spouse, however, at times, he travelled to join me.

I met Wayne in 1987 and we have been a complement

to one another ever since. I've never believed in finding a person to complete me or someone who liked everything I did. Some people describe Wayne and I as chalk and cheese; I describe us as Yin and Yang – always complementing and loving one another through the good and not so good times.

> **Throughout my life,
> I have found myself
> in beautiful places as
> well as very dark places.**

I have fought many dragons, but as the angels always tell me, it's important to rise to the challenge: Slay those dragons that appear in your life with LOVE and embrace them, for they always appear for your highest good! They also reminded me that we need the dark in order to appreciate the beauty of the stars in heaven above.

Recently, I have been asked how I bring light to the world. This is a very interesting and complex question to answer, however, I will give it my best shot.

> **We all have that internal light that
> makes us the special person that we are,
> but for some of us, the journey to find it
> is not always an easy one.**

I will give you some pointers that have helped me, because they may help you. First, is allowing the Creator/Higher Power to bring the message you need in order to brighten your own light, and in my humble opinion, allowing the angels into your life will be of great benefit.

> **I can hear you asking,
> 'But, how do I allow
> the angels into my life?'**

Firstly, our angels are always there for us from the time we are born, so simply, do not try and force the communication. Find a place that is comfortable for you (for me, it is in nature) and close your eyes. Breathe deeply.

Then, in your mind, invite the angels in. Do not judge your experience; simply surrender your mind, body and soul to them and become a conduit to receive their messages.

The angels will communicate with you through your thoughts, sounds, and experiences.

You may like to keep your eyes open or closed (it's up to you). The more you do this, the easier it will become to bring the angels into your daily life. You will see that you'll feel lighter and with a special glow that people will notice. This is one of the ways to allow your angels to bring light into the world, which I love and practice.

Another way I find very useful to bring light into the world is through healing. I, myself utilise a combination of Eastern and Western medicine.

As I got 'older and wiser', I began using Reiki and other energy healing modalities like Quantum Bioenergetics and Kinesiology.

All of these modalities tend to release energy which no longer serves us, and makes more room for the light that it was, once hidden behind all that rubbish we have been carrying for years; or some of us, from one lifetime to the next. These modes of healing help us to shine ever so brightly that we can feel it.

I have been very fortunate to allow my angels to always guide me to the best practitioner, who could assist me at any given point in time. I have been in a position to bring my light to so many different parts of the world in order to help healing for all concerned to take place, by simply shining my inner light with great determination compassion and love for everything and everyone. People's reactions of clear understanding of my energy and love was so evident to me. This blew my mind, but it was real. I was shining my light with unconditional love!

Remember shining our light also allows manifestation. Being able to shine your light and receive it back sometimes is hard, however, with a timely message via a friend offering a friendly ear or someone recommending a practitioner or touching your hand with love and compassion, and you accepting it, will determine what you will manifest.

The key component is shining your light through action from your part.

> **Angels will deliver many messages but they do respect your free will. To shine your light, you must also put hard work in yourself.**

It is not a simple task and it may take time, but with love, belief and perseverance, you can achieve it!

> **I found that writing has been a great vehicle for me to not only find my inner light at times when darkness over took me, but also to share my feelings, stories and lessons with others.**

Please remember that shining our light to the world, in my opinion, comes with great responsibility. We must write not only to help us heal but also to share with others that as a soul living a human experience, our Lightworker pathway has not been easy. Because of it, we can share those lessons with people that we will perhaps never meet, but our words can reach them at a very important point in their lives. I write to heal myself, to allow my light to shine bright – no apologies. It's similar to when you're told on an aeroplane to place the oxygen mask on yourself before helping others.

**I write to help heal others,
for the release you get
when you put pen to paper
(sorry, old school here).**

**It's an act of unconditional love;
regardless of the topic or how you feel.**

Writing helps us release, surrender, allow, love, grow and ultimately shine through our words. Please do not be judgmental when you write; let it flow out, there will be plenty of time later to edit. The important thing is honesty and love. That way, you will always shine! Becoming an author has been a great dream transformed into a magnificent reality, which took hard work and action from myself and others involved in order to manifest it.

**'What goes around comes around
so I decided to send LOVE!'**

Raúl Estévez, My Angels Connections

Throughout my life with friends and family, I have learnt that I am no longer a doormat to anyone just because I want them to love me. Also, in the last few years I have learnt there are a lot of people around you when times are great, but not so many when times are low. So, when people show me their true colours, I am not going to repaint them; meaning, I will no longer make excuses for them to justify their behaviour.

My angels have guided me through very tough circumstances in my life – some of them life threatening – but they have never forsaken me.

I am very happy with my journey as a Lightworker. I have met some amazing souls worldwide and I've become comfortable with my gifts as a psychic healer a 'Lightworker' who helps people achieve their dreams, and in turn they help me achieve mine.

I am a psychic and Angelic messenger who brings guidance from the Angels with Love, Compassion and Honesty.

Remember; Believe in Angels,
because they do believe in You!

Raúl Your Angelic Messenger

Raúl Estévez

Raúl Estévez, M.Ed., is an award winning Professional Educator, receiving the Vice Chancellor's Award for Teaching Excellence in the year 2000 at Victoria University in Melbourne Australia. He is an international Educator/Trainer, Psychic and Spiritual Healer, who has offered guidance, healing and mentorship to people worldwide.

He has helped people learn and achieve their full potential in Australia, Fiji, Malaysia, China, Singapore, Maldives, Tonga, Tuvalu, Vanuatu, Macau, Chile, Argentina, Colombia, USA and Canada. He holds a Master of Education from Melbourne University, as well as Quantum Bioenergetics Advanced Facilitator and is a Certified Angel Card Reader and Flower Therapy Healer by Doreen Virtue and Robert Reeves and a Peaceful Protection Facilitator by Robert Reeves. He is also a full member of the International Institute for Complementary Therapists.

In his first book 'My Angels – Connections', Raúl brings to the reader a set of short stories to inspire them to connect to their angels. His easy writing style allows the reader to truly connect at a heart, mind and soul level. In between stories you will find pages where Raúl encourages you to record you own connections with the Angels via your thoughts, dreams or intuition, it makes this book an interactive one. It has also been a wonderful experience where Raúl has been able to integrate his intellectual beliefs with his spiritual ones!

In his second Book 'My Little Angels Talk To Me' Raúl created a gorgeous Angelic stories to spark young minds imagination and also to encourage them to play outdoors with fun love and laughter. The book has beautiful illustrations by Sonia Darù, based on initial drawings by Raúl of the little angels. The book has an easy to carry handle and a section for kids to colour in their own version of the little angels and this section is perforated so they can easily detached their creations and display them.

Everything Raúl does is guided with the best intentions. He has a passion for helping people and he offers clear guidance from the heart. Raúl's two books are published by White Light Publishing House and they have also been accepted by Serenity Press to be showcased at the 'Meet the Author Event' at Crom Castle, Ireland and also at 'The London Book Fair' both in March 2017.

www.crystalbluebutterfly.com.au
https://m.facebook.com/raulestevezauthor/

Following the Light

By Karen Weaver

My name is Karen McDermott and I am the founder of Serenity Press and most recently, the Making Magic Happen Academy. I am an award winning entrepreneur and a proud mum of six healthy children aged from one to twenty. My business was founded with a desire of helping others share their story with the world. There is so much power in the written word. Words have the power to heal, comfort, empower and spread love especially when they are channeled through love. Let's face it, our world needs more love to spread around!

I first realised that I was a Lightworker when I became increasingly aware that my desire to help others in life was so intense that others around me couldn't comprehend why I would sacrifice so much of myself for the cause. I soon realised that the people around me didn't have the same urges. My immediate instinct is to help someone in need, it's an inbuilt program, I always give more than I receive. Everything I pursue is for a greater good and not financially motivated. I live through love and a passion or life; it's energising.

I have had a pretty good life. My childhood was filled with love and I have been blessed with lots of children to love. 2006 and 2007 were tough years for me and they instigated a change that I never thought I would ever follow through with. In 2006 I suffered from PTSD after an incident in my home. I had been numb to emotion for eighteen months and then in 2007 I endured a miscarriage. Even though it was early on in the pregnancy, it shook me to my core and I was devastated.

> **I discovered that through my pain and floods of tears was a positive; I felt alive, my soul had awakened and I could feel emotions again.**

I cried for my babies, I cried for the time I had lost and I prayed to be full again. Although my shining light was dimmed it was finally reignited!

It was through this dark time that I chose to move to Australia, and this is something that I will never regret. I could journey inside of myself and discover hidden treasures through which I could grow in spirit and heal with. I began to write.

Then it happened: I had the most profound euphoric moment when so many elements aligned and I felt compelled to write about my pain, my loss.

I felt compelled to share my realisation that I endured a miscarriage to awaken my soul and shift me back onto my right life path. It was for a reason. It was so empowering and I wanted other women to know it too and so I wrote The Visitor – a magical understanding of uncertainty in thirty days. Everything aligned to get this book published and I learnt so much about publishing. The ironic thing is that a quote at the front of my book was 'Through every negative situation there is the potential for a positive outcome.' I did not know then that the negative publishing experience I had would be a catalyst to me starting my own publishing press; it was like a training course as I learned every step of publishing. It was then that I researched printing houses only to discover that the very print and distribution network that was used for my book had opened up an office in Melbourne. Everything was aligned for me to make magic happen, and so I did.

Everything I do is with a loving intention. I will always stop along the way, no matter how busy I am, to help someone in need. What I learn can help someone else and if I can help then I will, and I will always help others share their stories and publish their books.

I don't connect with a specific entity however I am very in tune with my internal guide. When I focus on something, the answer finds me every time.

I have studied the Law of Attraction and I know the power that we all possess without even knowing it. We influence our existence every single moment.

I have a healing ability that I don't push too much. When my children are hurt I will sit with my hand over their graze and it heals in record time. My loving core pulsates and I know that my loving energy is healing them, and the love also heals the tears. I have had people approach me to ask if I would place my hands on their ailment. I know that through my presence I can shine a light in someone's day. I feel very blessed to have that ability.

I don't really identify any challenges about what I do. If there are any, I recognise that they are times of growth as I have something to learn in order to move forward. I am a passionate person who lives to inspire others through her work. I surround myself with positives and shield myself from negatives.

I am a philosophical thinker; I always think higher and wider than many other people. I remember when I was completing my creative writing course, feedback from my tutor stated that I was very philosophical in how I wrote. This was a huge compliment for me. When I write, I channel wisdom and love, and the story flows. My first book, The Visitor was meant to be written. I sat with my four-week-old baby and as she fed, I wrote. This book called to me to write it, and I have made many amazing friends through the like-minded souls I have connected with through it. It was a book that I healed through writing and it connects with people through the hidden wisdom that is weaved through the story.

My purpose in this lifetime is to share stories and books with the world – not just my own, but other peoples' as well.

Everyone has a story that is unique to them to tell. Nobody else can write that story; only them.

To anyone who is passionate about what they do: let your heart guide you. It is your internal beacon and has your truest intentions at its core. If you want to be successful, you will need to invest in yourself, and not just financially. Be resourceful and let your instinct guide you.

One of my favourite quotes is 'Where there is a will, there is always a way.' A quote that I wrote at the beginning of my The Visitor novel states: 'From every negative situation there is the potential for a positive outcome.' I live my true purpose; I am guided and I love everything I do. It is a great feeling that I recommend. Imagine if everyone honoured their true purpose; the world would be a happier place.

I hope that my story inspires you. You do not have to sacrifice yourself to be a Lightworker. Following your true purpose – the very thing that makes your heart sing – that is what you need to do.

With love, Karen x

Karen Weaver

Karen is passionate about the power of the written word and that everyone has a story to share. Her work focuses largely on shining love into our world.

She is an award-winning entrepreneur for her business Serenity Press and in 2017 she will be launching her Making Magic Happen Academy to help guide others towards living a magical life by accessing the Law of Love.

The most important thing in Karen's life are her six children, they light up her life every day. In her spare time she writes non-fiction, fiction and children's books. She is passionate about creating opportunities for Australian authors through Serenity Press and it is her mission to touch the lives of many people in a positive way.

Find out more about Karen:
www.facebook.com serenitypresspublishing
www.serenitypress.org

Photo courtesy of Monique Mulligan

Not Your Stereotypical
Lightworker

By Anna Peak

Ah, to be a Lightworker. At first I thought I was weird and different. Now I realise that I am not weird and I love being different. Different is a funny word for me to use though, because I see us all as the same; spiritual beings in physical form. We are all playing the perfect part here on Earth for our particular time-line. So in truth, none of us are really getting it wrong in life, I mean for me we are all a source of God's creation, so therefore we have the light of God in us all.

Okay, so maybe there are some people that choose to walk a path of destruction – harming other people, for example. I feel here that these people require more love, not less. Yes I said it. I get as angered and frustrated as the rest of the World when I see poverty, war and crimes against humanity. But in truth, we are all of the divine, it's just a matter of waking up to it. And I do believe that the grim times often bring moments of clarity, where people DO stop and think, they DO question. It is my belief that people are indeed waking up. People are coming together more and more, in times of grief. We are all in this together at this most special time here on Earth.

Do not get me wrong, are there lower vibrational energies attempting to prevent our mission of peace? ... maybe. We will all be of our own beliefs, but for me the focus has to be less on fear and more on love. A love revolution ... you can create your own you know, it's ace!

I am a Pleiadian, a Blue Ray. I am a healer. I pick up on people's energies wherever I go and my duty as a Lightworker is to transmute these energies of low vibration out of the collective. I would say that around ninety percent of what I actually feel is not my own 'stuff'! Before I knew that this was my role I would wonder why I would often collapse in a room full of people, become overwhelmed, panicked, sick, you name it.

**I am an empath, a clairvoyant
and I am telepathic.
I have seen/heard and
felt spirit from a very young age.**

However being so young I did not really understand anything about spirituality, I thought that I was seeing 'ghosts'. Maybe it was Angels, or my guides, who knows. But I used to see our cat that passed away regularly, I know that.

I grew up being frightened of what I saw and was told not to worry about it. 'You look like you've seen a ghost' came up many times!

I would try and ignore/block what I was experiencing, and this only made matters worse. Nothing I did worked. Our family home was built on an ancient thoroughfare, and I believe this to be the reason I would encounter various 'spirits' throughout my life. Perhaps they were attracted to my light, and perhaps some were up to mischief. We will never really know. All I know is that I had some not-so-nice experiences. I have been told as clear as day to 'get out of this house!' and several times I was growled at. I would also hear the laughter of children and a man playing his music, so it's not all bad. None of my friends would stay at my house though, oh no. The lady that 'tucked them in at night' saw to that!

One day I became so frightened that my father called on an 'expert'. I think the gentleman worked on TV as part of a ghost hunting production team and came recommended. When he got here he picked up on 'many spirits' and a portal in my bedroom. However on asking who spirit was 'there for', they insisted that they were there for my father. Miraculously, this is where my father admitted that he too felt/heard and saw 'spirit'. With this cleared up we could then be open and share our experiences. I felt better understood.

The years went on and my experiences became more frequent. But it was only when I turned 30 that my awakening happened. Without going into too much detail, my whole life I experienced panic attacks, fear, agoraphobia at times, anxiety and depression. This led to the overuse of alcohol in an attempt to mask what I was feeling.

I see now that I was blocking out my light and my true self.

I was standing in my flat one day and this feeling washed over me, very strong. I felt if I took one step further, something was going to happen. It did.

The doctor's termed it a 'nervous breakdown', and you can't blame them. But I see now that it was actually my breakthrough.

Once I had started to eat, walk, talk and function with a bit more ease I then found myself 'seeking'. The first thing I found myself seeking was someone to help me stop using alcohol as a mask. I was led to the right man.

I didn't know how or why but after two hours of specialised hypnotherapy I was free from alcohol. I did not desire it and even through the stresses and strains of life I have never thought of alcohol as an aid. I am still amazed, four years on. Not a drop has passed my lips and neither do I care.

The next thing I found myself led to was having an angel card reading.

I found a lady on the internet and gave her a call. To cut a long story short we had experienced almost the exact same things in life and we got on like a house on fire. She almost became my mentor. I was intrigued by what she had to say to me, her insights on me and her explanations as to what my past experiences meant for me – I am a Lightworker that had just experienced a Kundalini awakening.

It didn't take me long to fear Kundalini (I also kept this fear to myself which did not help – a word of advice if I may – do not believe and take in everything you read on the internet). With how I felt in going through this awakening, I was dreading this 'Kundalini' coming back. It is only now though, through experience and opening up about my fears that I realise that Kundalini is actually the energy there to 'save' you, not to harm you.

Kundalini, in a nutshell is a dormant energy that lies within most people.

It is depicted as (in Hindu mythology) a serpent goddess lay sleeping at the base of the spine. She is coiled three and a half times around our first chakra (root chakra) and she represents the unfolding of the divine Shakti energy; a living goddess who enlivens all things.

The Kundalini energy, under certain circumstances awakens and then starts to rise through the body. She moves up the body in a snake-like fashion piercing and opening each chakra as she goes.

The Kundalini releases all stored and blocked energies within you, and her movement can be quite intense and can lead to mental states that seem pretty much out of this world.

The circumstances that often stimulate Kundalini awakening are stress, trauma, extended periods of meditation, yoga, psychedelic drugs, fasting, near death experiences and meeting with soul mates and past life connections for example. However the circumstances can be many and varied.

Though the effects of Kundalini can sometimes be unpleasant, it is actually a healing force, and the effects may last for minutes, days, months or even years.

My Kundalini was kick-started when I first met my ex partner, not that I knew it at the time. The effects were strongly felt through my 'nervous breakdown' some years later and the Kundalini has now risen.

One of the signs that Kundalini had risen (for me) was seeing puffs of purple smoke when I close my eyes.

A Kundalini awakening is a multidimensional transformative process. Below is a list of just some of the symptoms that have been encountered:

- **Muscle spasms/twitches.**
- **Itching, stinging, 'crawling' sensations on the body.**
- **Headaches.**
- **Mystical experiences.**
- **Disturbed sleep.**
- **Ringing in the ears.**
- **Digestive system problems.**
- **Emotional outbursts/rapid mood shifts.**

- **Pains and blockages in the body – mainly in the back and the neck.**
- **Periods of extreme joy and bliss.**

So if you find yourself dealing with any of the above Kundalini awakening symptoms then some of my tips are as follows:

- **Get some support from someone who understands/has the knowledge/experience of Kundalini awakening.**
- **Lower stress.**
- **Help your body.**
- **Reduce/cut out nicotine, alcohol, caffeine and greasy foods for example.**
- **Treat underlying psychological issues, because Kundalini can bring up any unresolved issues to be dealt with.**
- **Practice 'grounding'. You can find many YouTube videos to help you with this. As the Kundalini is energy moving UP the body, in order to have greater balance it is a good idea to get grounded.**

Please do not allow 'awakenings' to become a fear for you. Everyone experiences something different and I have known a lot of people to 'awaken' very gently over time.

Although my awakening felt uncomfortable, I do realise in hindsight that I was being nudged, gently, for a very long time beforehand. I was clearly denying who I was (even if subconsciously) and it was time for me to wake up.

I had what is called a 'walk in'. This was not another soul entering my body; it was a newer version of me coming through, like a rebirth.

And we have all heard of growing pains. This is why I felt fearful of another awakening, because with my 'walk in' I was experiencing what many would go through over a period of time, at once. I had to awaken. I am a first waver. My participation in co-creating change on this planet was required. It's what I signed up to do.

First wavers are often referred to and thought of as the next step in human evolution, in mindset and frequencies.

They constitute the revolution for the evolution of our species and planet.

> **First waver is basically a term that is used to define a 'wave' of people that have contracts that have been activated! The contracts involve assignments, and once fulfilled they will further the mission of ascending Earth and her inhabitants.**

First wavers, for the most part, have been 'awake' for some time, and the activations that we receive now are to perform the tasks agreed upon in support of the ascension of the planet. We either work directly with our spirit guides or indirectly through groups associated with our mission.

It is of my understanding that the First Wavers' contracts were activated in the year 2000, and that there will be a second and third wave yet to come. In fact, I think there was a mass awakening just recently.

The contract, to my knowledge, is a contract for ascension teaching and leadership.

Basically, we are preparing the world for transition. A first waver could be an inventor who creates the technology that will be needed in the future for example. He or she could be a teacher of the concepts of multidimensionality.

They are the teachers and assistants for all steps on the ascension path. Think of the ascension process as like a staircase. There will be teachers on each step that enable the people on the planet to move along the path and complete each step, one at a time.

So going back to the lady I found on the internet, it was from here that I was led to a meditation course, and thereafter an Angelic Reiki workshop.

I promise you I sat down in that room, looked around and thought what on earth am I doing here? Angels?

And before I could think about it the workshop had begun. I have never experienced anything like it. Angels exist, I thought to myself. Oh my God, I thought to myself.

My hands shone blue, my body moving as the Angels and Archangels directed me through the healings. I still struggle to explain how amazing I felt. Over time, the 'struggle' of the awakening becomes more of a blessing.

I will not say that my life has been easy, but you know what, whose life has? I doubt you would find even one awakened soul that will paint you all carebears and rainbows. This is not to sound like a victim, as I have experienced and continue to experience incredible things, all the time.

The important thing to mention here is that without a struggle or two, a broken heart or two, how would we be able to carry out our work? How could we possibly help those that are awakening around us? It is in my opinion that we would not know what to say or how to deal with it.

Let's also not be afraid to discuss the fact that being 'spiritual' does not necessarily mean you are nice, empathic and friendly all the time. We are human.

I've met some spiritual people along the way that see this path as a battle ground– who can be more spiritual? 'Well I meditate 23 hours a day'. I mean come on, are we not trying to clear this type of energy out of the collective? Are we not all one? More love not less. To those people I bless and send love, but I do not see myself as above them.

Some want to jump 'ahead' ... jump ahead to what I am not quite sure. We are all on the same boat, no matter how long you have been on the spiritual path. I have met people who have asked me what I am complaining about, that they have been on the path for 30 years and deserve their enlightenment before me.

When I hear this I simply think to myself maybe that's why you're still looking?

There is no end.
Live in the moment and love.

We are infinite beings and if you are thinking you have done your time, join the club. That to me actually means you still have some learning to do! (can you tell I do not sugercoat?)

By the way, I am NO Mother Theresa. My challenges on this path have included anxiety, depression, substance abuse, nervous 'breakdown', relationship breakdown, 'starting over completely' twice already by the age of 34, bullying, self loathing and of course not forgetting loneliness.

Loneliness is common. When something is not in your best interest it can get stripped away. You will have warnings mind you, gentle nudges, but me being me I tend to drag along by the fingernails, stubbornness in hand. Eventually I will have to admit defeat and 'let go'.

'Let go', now let me tell you how I feel about 'let it go' ... you will hear this often. For me, I hate hearing those words. One simply cannot just let go. My feelings cannot be lifted and popped into a bucket.

Maybe each of us just interpret it differently and I need to get off my high horse, but what I see it as is looking at what is causing you the fear/anxiety you are experiencing (whether it be a relationship, work issue etc) and sit with those feelings.

I allow myself to feel the feeling as best I can and then I will thank those feelings and say 'I allow you to pass'.

Different things work for different people. For me, to constantly clear and cleanse everything is like telling yourself there is something wrong with you. I don't get it. However do not get me wrong, healing definitely has its place for me. I see healing as actually awakening, not like healing a boil on my backside.

The more I use Angelic Reiki on someone the more they wake up to who they truly are, so they can see that in truth there is nothing TO be healed.

How I promote and bring change to this world is by allowing people to speak their truth. You cannot bang on about your spiritual path to someone who does not have a clue what you are talking about. They will not suddenly wake up and thank you for your efforts.

For me it is about 'hearing' people. Compliment, compliment, compliment. More love, less judgement (easier said than done I understand!! We are human after all).

And you know what, even if you do make a judgement that is ok too. So what if you had a THOUGHT about someone taking too long with their coupons at Asda. Why we insist on punishing ourselves I do not know.

I also like to celebrate my uniqueness as much as my personality will allow. It is ok to be spiritual, to be you.

**It took me so long to come out of the
spiritual closet that by the time I did
I thought I do not care what anyone
says about it anymore!
I wasted all my energy on fearing it,
never mind what anyone else thinks.**

Do I wave my spirituality around like a banner, like I am different? No. We are one, as far as I am concerned. However I am human and I do look back on my life at the times where I felt alone, like I did not matter to many. Eventually I realise oh! That's it! It's because those people HAD to go away, it's because I AM actually part of something unique, and other people I know do not have that. They are asleep. Wow, go me. I know, oops, but sometimes I do pat myself on the back for being the spiritual warrior that I am.

What better way to bring change to humanity (whether you see it first hand or not) than to bless everything in sight. Every day I bless people. Driving down the road and I see the postman – 'may you be blessed'. Not only have you blessed that person but the love will ripple out and WILL be felt by many, including you.

I listen to people and I am a giver. I am still learning to receive (many will find it very easy to give but not to receive – even if it's just a compliment).

I pray for people and the World. I do not do what many do and purposely avoid the news. For me (in my truth) I feel like I am denying reality or pretending it does not exist. Well it does, so I bless the person/situation I see and I make it my intention not to dwell on it. This is hard being an empath.

**No human being on this spiritual path
is the same. What works for some
may not work for others.
What you feel comfortable with
is your truth. Remember that.**

And I know we always hear when the student is ready the teacher will appear, but my advice would be not to see yourself as an eternal student. There came a time where I started declaring that I am the Master of my life. I co-create my reality.

Advice is fantastic but ultimately we have to make our own choices.

In my life I have worked as a teacher, an animal care worker, an administrator and then I had the nervous 'breakdown'. As I was feeling ready to dip my toe in the water again, my long-term partner left me out of the blue. I received no explanation and I am still none the wiser. I have to forgive someone that I adored that is not even sorry.

I have taken the time to grieve, to feel the anger, the pain, rejection and dis-ease and I am now a lot stronger. I see the blessings now.

I am now two months into a volunteer role and I am looking for part time work. I will never give up helping people and spreading the love.

I am sure my parents' would have wanted a doctor or a lawyer, but I have never been able to 'do' something I did not want to do without the universe stepping in.

Many people strive to find their 'purpose', and I am only just learning that your purpose is to follow your joy.

What if your purpose was to be a loving mother? What if your purpose was to be a great friend? Your joy is your purpose, because where there is joy there is love, and love heals all.

I do not have a particular 'faith'. For me there is one God/Creator/source, and why we are all here doing what we do, why we have to evolve, why we want to experience everything life has to offer (if you believe in reincarnation), well I do not believe that anyone knows the exact answer to that. I do not think we are meant to.

All I know is that love is the answer. Love is the key.

When I hear people say 'you have one life, make the most of it', I silently chuckle to myself. It is my belief that I have had many. And if I am not concerned with climbing the ladder to CEO then maybe that is because I did that 20 times already!

Sometimes I wish I did not have to be on the spiritual path, and with that statement I do not intend to scare anybody. It is beautiful and touching and an absolute blessing, but like many, you may feel that it can be a curse at times; to feel things so deeply, to feel misunderstood.

Not everyone is going to understand you. Of course we all have many soul mates in our family and friends, but in terms of feeling understood, I am yet to feel one of many as opposed to 'the spiritual one', 'the weirdo' or 'the psychic'. My tribe will come, and I do have like-minded friends to call upon.

Enjoy the ride, because I think that is the one thing that we are supposed to be doing but are yet to achieve (fully).

Whether I feel good or I feel put upon, I will always sing it out ... 'I'm sad, but I am the bestestttt, the bestessssst at being saaaaad, yes I am yes I am yes I AMMMMM, I am the bestest in the world at being SAAADDDD ... AMEN!' Turning the negative into a positive can actually shift the energy. Again, this is easier said than done.

If ever you feel like you do not know what you are doing (like we all have, MANY times), I will always say 'OK, Universe, I do not know what I am doing, so please work through me, for me'.

There are no rules on how to be spiritual. You just are. So spread your love, hope and joy however best suits YOU. Do not let anyone tell you how to live. I was once told that having thoughts was a bad thing, and until I got rid of those thoughts then my ego would always be in charge. Look, I have thoughts, and so what?

For me, I think that thoughts are just the universe weighing up every possibility. The only person judging your thoughts is YOU. And as for the ego, so what if we have one – make friends with it I say! Thank the ego for the thoughts and proceed with love.

**If you ever find yourself afraid,
what I do is call on Archangel Michael
(the Angel of protection)
and I ask him to be by my side
and help me.**

He always will.

I think that it is important to accept that we cannot be in charge of everything. There is so much you may 'learn' or hear about on this path. You may hear that you must be grounded – yes, very helpful, that you should keep your heart open – yes, helpful, that you should know what to do because you are spiritual, and you should be nice and know why you are here and create world peace!!! ... I know you detect my sarcasm! Just breathe. Nobody is perfect, everything is in Divine timing and everything is here to help you.

I would like to thank each and every one of you reading this for your contribution to this Planet. You are valued and important.

May you be blessed, and one last thing, I love you.

Anna

Anna Peak

My name is Anna Peak and I am an empathic psychic clairvoyant as well as an Angelic Reiki Master Teacher. I give psychic readings to my family and friends, and others that approach me via recommendation. I enjoy working alongside the Angelic Kingdom in bringing healing to individuals. I offer this service to anyone around the world that should approach me via email.

I have been on the spiritual path for many years and know myself well. I have been through many life experiences that have helped shape the person I am today. Through my experiences I can relate and show empathy to those that require a listening ear and a helping hand.

I am from the United Kingdom and my passions include helping people and animals in any way I can, healing, sports, teaching and leading. It is my intention that you find some comfort in my story, something to laugh along with and something to give you hope.

allthingsangels@hotmail.com

The Spiritual
Truth

By Elizabeth Inglis

My desire to be a Lightworker has always been consciously on my mind, even when I'm subconscious in my sleep! I was teased at school for being 'different' and I always knew that I was different. I have come across my challenges and obstacles in my path, but I have always persisted and rise above them...every single one of them. You can do the same, my friend!

So what is a Lightworker? Everyone has their own personal interpretation of what a Lightworker is. For me personally, it's about being a service to others and giving a positive insight on life, even when there doesn't seem to be light at all sometimes. But without the darkness, how do each of us now that there's light? We need to sometimes experience darkness in order to experience the light! Nevertheless, there is always and forever light than darkness. Everyone is a Lightworker, even you the wonderful reader reading this! It doesn't require any particular skills or knowledge, but rather one simple act of kindness. When you are kind to someone else, even a complete stranger, you not only feel better for it, but you change the world with one simple act of compassion, of respect, of non-judgement, to help someone else in need. It's a part of being a human being, not just a Lightworker.

This is my own philosophy to helping our world. If we look at the soul – everyone has a beautiful soul, within their psyche.

If we look at the soul, rather than the person – we will discover that each of us, is equal in the eyes of the Divine and all the realms of love and light.

I was born with mild Cerebral Palsy, and I knew about my own limitations…physical limitations, but I didn't realise my own inner potential with myself. My family has always been supportive, loving and encouraging with everything I do. But I never realised my 'inner' power, my 'inner' being until I was an adult. While, I have had limitations and challenges, I have always persevered even if things didn't go exactly how I thought they would. I have come to realise that everything happens for a reason, and it's either a lesson – a learning experience and a blessing.

I have always been fascinated with World Religions, and I really did excel particularly well within Catholic school. I just loved gaining knowledge and wisdom through learning. I have always loved learning…and I was always willing to have a go, even at mathematics! Okay, I just past mathematics in Year 11!

The journey towards embracing spirituality has been an interesting one. Since I was a child, I heard voices, but for years I thought they were truly in my head. For years, I thought there was something seriously wrong with me. I also saw lots of colour, particularly the beautiful colours blue, green and pink. Now, I truly realise that these colours were of the Divine beings of light and love: Archangels Michael, Raphael and Ariel! These beloved Archangels are my guardian angels always protecting and guiding me. I can channel many deities of the Divine. I strongly connect with Angels, Archangels, Guardian Angels, Spirit Guides, Spirit Animals, Ascended Masters, as well as the Saints in Christianity. These beautiful celestial beings of God (or however you see God and there are many different names of God or the Higher Source), only give me very uplifting and positive messages.

I grew up in a traditional Catholic household and I was taught that spirituality was strange or weird; nevertheless it is very important to respect all world religions, and this touched upon spirituality. I also had a very deep fascination with people who had psychic abilities – I loved that people had the abilities to hear, see, touch, smell, feel or just know about something or someone. In a sense, I thought I couldn't have these abilities until I started chatting and encountering people who were psychics. I was flabbergasted to be told that I was indeed one of their own!

How could I be psychic? Let me answer that question, by saying that EVERYONE has psychic abilities! We all have them, and have the abilities to open that door to a world of possibilities of spiritual potential. It is truly the spiritual truth that is in every single human being on this planet. It is a special group that each of us can be a part of. Everyone has the ability to channel and tap into their own psychic and spiritual abilities. We all have them, no one isn't without them.

With my own journey, I started reading books, and taking online courses, the more I learnt about spirituality – and yes, there's plenty to learn – the more I had learnt about this topic; the more I fell in love with it, and this truly felt like my life purpose, and that was wonderful! I had found my own tribe of like-minded people that I can always depend on. I even decided to start my own business, since I felt intuitively guided to do so.

There are some challenges about being a Lightworker, but I do have to say with my own experiences, the majority has been very positive. Some people might express their opinions or they believe it's weird or strange, but while they are entitled to their opinion, so am I.

Some people (not everyone) do often ask you to channel for them because they are sceptical of your abilities, and sometimes they with you to 'test' you to see if you get things wrong or right. If this happens to you, fellow Lightworker, please do not worry.

Surround yourself with pink light of the Divine Love. You can still listen and respect other people's opinions or thoughts, but use your own inner wisdom, and intuition to speak your own truth in a respectful way, but you own your own truth.

My life purpose for this current life is to help others, to be a service to others. I feel very strongly guided to help others find their own life purpose in a very spiritual, psychic and holistic approach to life. I do see myself as a spiritual teacher, healer and author. We are all here for a reason, right here, right now.

Everyone has their ups and downs through their life, but when each of us works together, and helps one another, we make our world a better place.

Each of us is always learning, and even I, I love learning new things. The Master always teaches the student, but in return, the student teaches his or hers Master as well!

So dear friends, even when life may give you any form of limitations, or trauma or challenges, please remember that in spiritual truth – we are limitless; we are always connected to the Divine, to God, to Love, to the Universe.

The more you give out to the Universe with the highest intentions of love and light, you will get some form of abundance in return. You are always compensated through the law of attraction, with the highest love that you can ever imagine. As the great Beatles' song 'All you need is Love' is very true to each and every one of us. With love and light and many Angel blessings to you, always.

Elizabeth Inglis (Libby)

Elizabeth Inglis
Libby is psychic medium, angel and Tarot card reader, Reiki and Crystal Therapy Practitioner.

She is passionate about helping others learning about their own spiritually journey. Libby is a life long learner and enjoys reading, writing and playing her violin.

If you would like to contact Libby, please go to her website:
www.blessingsbylibby.blog
or you can find her on Facebook:
https://www.facebook.com/blessingsbylibby

Tale of an
Indigo Scout

By Ellen D Merritt

I dare say that each of us in the Rainbow tribe are born knowing that we are different. I came along in December of 1965. I was supposed to be born in February of 1966. Nowadays, medical science has made a habit of saving premature infants, including those born at 24 weeks. Back then, being born at 28 weeks was an almost certain death sentence. My mother, a conservative Christian, prayed and asked God to spare me. In return, she would dedicate my life to God's service. I am alive and kicking, and firmly in the service of the Most High. Just in a rather unusual way.

Childhood was excruciating for me. Prematurity had left me with several health problems and developmental disabilities. I was bullied and rejected by my peers. I realize that many children and teens suffer from the cruelties of peers for one reason or another and I am grateful now for these past experiences. Because I know that pain, I can relate to the pain of others in a similar situation and be able to help them cope with it in a healthy manner. Like I could not at the time.

I liked broccoli. I used my birthday money to send Christmas stockings to kids in the Philippines when I was six. I wanted to read about every culture on Earth as well as every biography I could get my hands on. I never waited for the teacher's instructions. I asked my Daddy at age nine if there was life on Mars. I wanted to know exactly what happened when we died. I hated recess because I was pushed aside, ignored, teased. I trusted no one and much preferred to be alone. My favorite spot was a special branch of a mulberry tree in our back yard where I would climb up and sit with the book du jour, reading for hours. Mom insisted that I be a cheerleader in elementary school. Any girl who wanted to join was accepted. I never could do a cartwheel or a split. Still can't. I was in Girl Scouts. I went to church twice on Sunday and on Wednesday night. I was in the youth group.

I tried to do what girls my age should like to do. I could not seem to fit in.

I did love to write and wrote my first play at age six or seven for the Girl Scouts, as I recall. It was about pollution and the importance of protecting our environment. In our fourth grade play, I was one of a couple of kids who wanted to be a hero. All the other kids fought over which villain they wanted to portray. We two would-be heroes were labeled as 'weird' and abandoned. I got the part of Valiant. I don't remember a single line of that play but I loved that part.

At the age of ten, I remember sobbing to a teacher on the playground, 'I feel like an alien!' And I did. I wondered what was wrong with me.

My younger sisters seemed to have little trouble getting along with the other children. I knew that things the other kids raved about: boys, clothes, makeup, movie stars, TV shows, etc. were superficial and temporary. My mind was on much bigger things.

> **I avoided peer relationships as much as possible because I had been hurt so much; yet at the same time, I craved acceptance and tried to do just about anything to get it.**

At 17, I went on a youth mission trip to Glorieta, New Mexico with the youth group from my uncle's church. For the first time, I found myself in a group of peers who liked and accepted me for who I was. And I received a Call to Missions. At last I had a purpose for my life. I had always been under pressure, as the 'miracle child', to do something great with my life. Well, this was something great to do for God and I knew my mom would be proud. Accordingly, I prepared for Seminary after college graduation and went to Louisville Kentucky. I thought I would serve as a Southern Baptist missionary. However, due to interdenominational conflict and the onset of what I would discover was bipolar disorder, I was forced out of school with one semester to go in a three year program. Everything was gone. I wished I was dead. And I was in and out of the hospital for years.

> **For years, I foundered, lost and in an existence of despair.**

I tried building a career. I tried to become a mother and start a family. I tried anything that might give me a purpose. Everything failed.

In 1998, I was alone in the house, taking a break from preparing to care for my father in law, who was recovering from bypass surgery. He was a brilliant mathematician who had worked designing nuclear submarines. I had fallen in love with Star Wars years earlier and was fascinated by the Jedi. I thought that we might be able to design a working lightsaber as a project. We had just gotten an Internet connection and I did a Google search. To my astonishment, there were several online communities which actually trained Jedi Knights! One of these, the Force Academy, became my home and in training, I discovered that I had several abilities: empathy, telepathy, energy healing, reading people, seeing auras, linking with the energies of others, spiritual warfare (actually fighting Dark forces) and so on. I trained finally with a mage and learned more about spirit guides, the Upper and Lower worlds, shielding, energy manipulation and healing, Binding and interaction with beings of all kinds.

I eventually earned the title of Light Jedi Master and led an international Council of people who called themselves Jedi.

We wrote lecture after lecture for training materials covering such topics as the Force, the Jedi Code, leadership, service, anger management, self awareness, meditation, physical fitness and spirituality. Not to be confused with religion. I worked with professionals in the fields of education and health care to develop a formal training program for real-life Jedi. And I used this program as the capstone project for my Master's degree in Psychology. I trained people as Jedi and loved helping those with special abilities to develop and use these Gifts properly and to find and follow their own path.

Shortly after this, I met an archangel in meditation whom I believed was Michael, but have since been informed that it was Metatron. This being telepathed, 'You have a great destiny' and disappeared. I have not seen him since but these words have stayed with me. I met my birth totem, Owl, who took me to meet with a Triune Goddess I know as the Lady. She gave me a pot of healing salve and I saw that She is the same Being of Light and love as the God I have served all my life. Yes, we've met. In the Throne Room.

**I saw this dazzling Light
and felt unconditional love.**

I sat on the Being's lap for a while and finally felt the love and acceptance I had always wanted and needed but never got except from my parents.

It gets weirder. I was made a Paladin, the first female Paladin in 1200 years, as I was given to understand. As a Paladin of the Book, I helped to guard the Akashic Records for over a decade. I also continued to fight demonic forces and complete various assignments from the Boss. After my encounters with the Lady and the Most High, I knew for a fact that the human mind cannot comprehend or classify the Divine. I started calling this being 'the Boss' because I work for Heaven and get assignments frequently. Eventually, my health declined precipitously and I laid down my Paladin sword for good.

**It took me a while to realize
why my health had failed.
We are all connected at many levels.
And when I harmed others,
I harmed myself.**

I had known about the Force binding everything together for years and had reached personal conclusion that the Force and the Holy Spirit were one and the same. I call myself a Christian Jedi. But I only had head knowledge before this. Now I have heart knowledge.

I started using social media and discovered that many people are starting to awaken spiritually. I became aware that I am actually a being known as an Indigo Scout and a part of the Rainbow tribe. With this piece of the puzzle, my life started to make sense. Indigo Scouts like me came to see whether the world is ready for the next step and, deciding it was, we started clearing the way for the Crystal children (several of whom came to the Jedi to learn more about their unique gifts) and the new Rainbow children. I have recently written and published a workbook to help people determine what they want and how to get where they want to go. I wish I had had this years ago. It is called 'Break Free and Move Forward' and is available through Amazon. I wrote it for you, so you can blaze your own trail in a world that has become much more accepting of us Lightworkers.

I am continuing to help anyone, Jedi or not, who are awakening and in need of direction and instruction. And of course, I welcome any instructions from the Boss. I have watched happily as children have had access to education which allows them to be free to nurture every aspect of themselves. I have looked with pride as my Spirit children have overcome obstacles and challenges to achieve their dreams and goals

And, for as long as I am on this Earth, I will continue to shine my Light on the edge of the cliffs so that others can avoid falling over the edge.

I am a servant of the Most High. I am a Guardian. I am a Christian Jedi. I am an Indigo Scout in the Rainbow tribe. I am a Lightworker. And I have done a great deal during my life thus far. And you can do greater things.

So who will you be? What will you do to shine?
We Indigos are watching and cheering you on!
We know that we are leaving the world in
good hands.

Ellen Merritt

Ellen Merritt

Ellen Merritt has been involved in spirituality all her life. In recent years, she has been delighted to find her 'tribe'. Her article, 'Tales of an Indigo Scout' recounts some of her personal journey.

Ellen has always best expressed herself through writing. She wrote her first play at the age of six and her writings can be found on Facebook, Twitter, Scriggler and in two anthologies published from Centum Press.

She has been active in writing teaching materials for the Jedi Realist community since 1998.

A Little Bit of
Heaven on Earth

By Julia Van Der Sluys

I am lucky that I have been a Lightworker of sorts for eons of years, since the dawning of time, I guess you could say. The last 36 years I have been blessed with having a human body to do this precious work of the Lightworker.

It isn't always the easiest of jobs, the lessons that you need to learn in order to help others can be tough, can take you to the darkness and beyond, can test your faith and everything you stand for. Yet I wouldn't trade it for anything. The joy of someone's AHA moment, the connections with Spirit in all of its form and beyond, the messages you get to pass on – there are so many more joyous moments of being a Lightworker that far outweighs the darker times.

I am a Guardian Angel, I used to identify it as being separate to me, being that at the moment I am walking Earth on two feet for the first time, but it is what I essentially am, it is my soul, it is wholly who I am – regardless of being shelled in human form. With this brings a unique skill set which I use to empower others, to heal and to bring to light information needed for humanity as a whole.

> **My energy seems to help those
> I come into contact with,
> no matter if it is with only a smile
> as they pass or a conversation,
> to a healing.**

Being a newbie Earthling has brought it's own set of challenges, throw in the mix, what I have come here to learn – means life hasn't been easy, especially when I have hung on to that old way of being for so long.

Things can get overwhelming – experiencing things for the first time, doing things, trying things – I have very much felt like the toddler learning to take its first steps many times over in this life. It can especially be interesting when I remember that I have watched this from above so surely it has to be easy – until you actually try and realise that that is certainly not always the case.

> **Growing up was hard,
> part of my lesson was to learn
> why humans always seemed
> to take the negative, ego approach
> to life so of course the start of life
> had to be difficult to experience that.**

A broken home, an alcoholic parent, sexual abuse, bullying and much more were in store for me. I also never fit in, looking back I can see it was probably a sub-conscious realisation that

I was very different from them and they didn't quite know how to take me. Plus my essence I presume attracted much unwanted attention that I just didn't know how to deal with back then. From coming from a pure loving, peaceful place that always is high vibrational, no matter what, stepping into this life was a huge eye opener and something I realised as soon as I entered the womb where I had a moment of 'Holy crap, what was I thinking?!'

All of that accumulated into a very low esteemed, acute panic disorder sufferer with an eating problem, that just couldn't deal, couldn't cope with everyday life and it meant that I checked out for much of my life – just existing and thinking that was enough.

> **I was trapped inside a mental cage
> that I had created myself,
> with no way of knowing
> how to open that door
> until the time was right
> and the people,
> circumstances and opportunities
> started coming together for me
> and basically my own spiritual pit crew
> gave me a slap upside
> the head and basically said
> enough is enough.**

That time is over, waaayyyy over, you have learnt what you needed to and now it is time to let those wings unfurl and be what you are truly meant to be doing here. I am an empath as well so it made it even harder, but with simple shielding, boundaries and cutting of the cord techniques, has made it easier to live on a day to day basis. Just asking yourself the question of 'is this mine' is an excellent way of working out what is and isn't yours. And even if that low vibe is yours, never fear – Michael is here. I use him constantly throughout the day to cut away anything that does not belong to me and any low vibe stuff that does.

**That is why I know how to
help someone slowly crawl out
of that deep dark pit they
created for themselves.
I know how it is to stay in a
victim mentality and have to
take responsibility for
what is happening in life.**

I also know the sheer joy of working through something and getting that freaking awesome aha moment. To knowing that all this was worthwhile because now I can help others and also take my learnings back to the Angelic Realm.

It is knowing that sometimes stuff happens to give you a side shuffle, but that it is okay and you are honestly at each moment in time – the best you can be and that is freaking okay!

Being a Guardian Angel – I can tap into previously unchartered territory, calling on someone's Guardian Angel for healing and messages.

**Healing Voices is an amazing
channelled voice recording where
I allow someone's, or my own,
or even Archangels to use
my voice to record a healing.**

It is a recording of noise, tonings and singing (it really is indescribable until you have heard it) that brings deep healing and recognition of what they need to work on for long lasting change, it is really phenomenal! Angels are definitely my forte being that they are my family but I call myself, which my mentor shakes her head at, a spiritual dabbler. I try everything and can do all things, some better than others and some I do for a time before mastering and knowing it is time to move on. I can access other realms and I can step in to souls, which believe me, scared the bejesus out of me when I first did it! My skills are always changing and evolving the more I let go and do what they ask me to do, the more I step in my Angelic side. As a close friend would say, I am Gods Earthbound right hand woman, a walking Guardian Angel who is reinforcing Jesus' work and taking it to the next level – not much to live up to is it?!! I truly have connections to all 'beings', to all skills, and if I need help in any way, my spiritual pit crew go out quick smart and get what I need to master it. I take each day as it comes, I take my skills each day as they show up. I know some of my future and it is WOW but I also don't focus on it, because that would be daunting as hell and make me wonder if I can live up to it, which is my little Ego monster raising its head because of course I can! See even Lightworkers have those moments. And it is those moments that I capture in blogs and posts.

It is not all about acting as if life never has any hiccups, it is about showing that you can still have them and have a fabulous life, and I feel it is my role as a Lightworker to bring these out in my unique voice to give hope, to inspire and to maybe bring about evolvement to whoever reads and watches me.

It can sometimes be about bringing those Ego moments to life and giving them a positive twist and definitely the lesson! It can also just be talking about the magicness of Spirit in all of its wonderful glory.

I also do readings – Intuitive and Psychic Readings, Medium, Animal Spirit and Guardian Angel readings – those are my favourite as I connect with ones Guardian Angel and give them the name, colours, Archangel they are under and any messages they want to pass on. However, my greatest work is through my Angelic Healing Voices. I am far from the many gifted in this world. My uniqueness, that I am a Guardian Angel, brings through information, signs, sounds, visions and messages that, to date, is non comparable to others. Having direct access to all past, present and future worlds, universes and galaxies allows me the privilege of calling myself the Magician of all readers.

Most importantly I bring a little bit of 'heaven' to Earth and to those I come into contact with.

Think a touch from Jesus, a warm hug from Mary and Wings wrapping around to give you that warm, safe, loved feeling that your soul knows intimately.

To hold your hand, as you find your way back to the true you and spirit with a bit of Angel magic.

I wasn't brought up with a religion of any kind – but I was always drawn to churches when I could visit them. Jesus, Mary, the Angels etc. that were depicted always drew me in and gave me goose bumps and such an amazing feeling. Now that I am older, there are many philosophies that I enjoy bits and pieces of but nothing that I practice in depth. While I believe and love all things God, Jesus and the bible, I do not prescribe to the way some humans have deciphered the bible to their way of thinking. As more and more of the past lives that I have guided come back to me – I definitely believe in the stories and people from the Bible, when once I may have been a bit dubious as to what went on back then, I can't now that I have had an aerial front seat to them. It just hurts to see so many use it as an excuse for war and hate when that is so far from the truth of what it is all about – love for all and peace and joy, to come from that spiritual space rather than Ego. I love the Buddhist approach to life and their philosophy, it really resonates with me. I am a typical Gemini though where it all interests me and I dabble in all different things from time to time but do not go deeply into it and practice it religiously.

**One of my biggest mantras that
I want you to remember and
keep in your heart, is you are ok
EXACTLY as you are, right here,
right now, in this time and
space exactly as you are.**

You do not need to change or fix anything. You are perfect exactly as you are. Is there room for evolvement? Absolutely! But that does not mean there is anything wrong with you. There is always something to work on, let go or evolve too. It does not mean that where you have been, are or doing is wrong.

**It is just simply where you are at,
right in this moment in time.
Everything happens for a reason,
everything has its time and place.**

Sure we sometimes hang on to things for too long and it means that the lesson has been a super hard and long one, but only because we created it, because we have gotten stuck a little too much in our Ego and decided to let it take the driver's seat. And that is totally okay too.

**It is about loving the shadows
as well as the light that true
transformation can occur.**

Just be you, just allow Spirit (God, universe, all the good stuff) into your life daily and come from that space, that loving, all knowing peaceful/positive space that you truly are at soul level. And excuse my language, but rejoice in your shit! Where you have been, where you are at, who you are, has been brought about from ALL of your experiences, good and bad.

It has made you YOU! And honestly, what has happened and come about from any bad (or good) experience – you have the capacity and the control to change it.

You have created everything in your life, whether from things that happened to you or by you. So grab your life by the hands, stand up strong and in your power and own ALL of you. Because you my darling are MAGNIFICENT, or as I always say – AMAZEBALLS.

And just remember to bring Love, the Light and Hope into your life every day, in any way that you can. And remember that Spirit in all of its glory, totally has your back, you only have to allow it.

Julia Van Der Sluys

Julia is a psychic, intuitive medium and healer, for both humans and animals. She is a published author and is here to share her knowledge of what she has seen and learnt viewing earth, from Gods' side, as a Guardian Angel.

She is here to show you how to connect to the almighty and in a way that will uplift, inspire and spread love in all and every soul she comes in contact with.

Her story on the lives/souls that she protected, healed and helped, to pass over, is what she is here to share with the world. She has been sent to earth to be Gods' right hand, earthbound Guardian Angel.

You can find her here:
https://www.facebook.com/ariabellarises/
https://yellowwolfenlightenment.wordpress.com/
http://ariabellarises.wixsite.com/ariabellarises

Guided by
Love and Light

By Michelle Beber

I am both humbled and honored to be a Lightworker. I can't think of anything I'd rather do than help others to live a better life with the messages I've received from the angels. My connection to the angels is relatively new. About 13 years ago, I went through a very tumultuous period that led to a spiritual awakening – a realization that the three-dimensional world is only a part of our reality. After this epiphany, I grew by leaps and bounds, learning everything I could about spirituality. I was on my way to remembering who I really was and discovering why I was here.

My journey began very unexpectedly at a very low point in my life. In 2003, I was under a tremendous amount of stress, extremely depressed, and going through what I now know was the 'dark night of the Lightworker's soul'. I yearned to be able to hug my mom one more time and have her tell me everything would be okay. My mom had died 17 years earlier, and I had recently found comfort watching a famous psychic medium's television show. The messages from the afterlife made me feel like there was a possibility my mother might still be around me.

One day, after watching the medium's show, I decided to look through an old photo album to reminisce about happier times with my family, especially my mom. When I proceeded to put the photo album away, a photo fell on the floor. When I looked down, I saw a picture of my mom looking up at me and smiling. It was as if she was right there with me at that very moment. I felt it in my heart and soul, but I wouldn't have it officially validated until five years later when I went to the Conscious Life Expo in Los Angeles, California to see a renowned psychic medium.

It was there that I was among the fortunate few who would receive an impromptu reading. It was an unbelievable and emotional turning point in my life.

My mom came through with the personality I knew, and I was told specific details only my mom would've known. It was very clear to me that my mom wasn't dead and that the connection I had with her was real.

I started to research everything I could about after-death communication, which is direct and spontaneous contact from a deceased loved one without the use of a medium. This intuitive communication can be visual, auditory, or something you just know or feel. As I believed in the connection between my mom and me, I would receive signs from her on a regular basis.

When I started to understand that we are spiritual beings living inside human bodies, it completely changed my life.

**I awakened to my truth and
the truth of everyone else here on Earth.
I knew that my life purpose was to
awaken others and let them know
that our loved ones never die,
that we stay connected through love,
and that we receive signs that
our loved ones are still with us.**

As I strengthened my continuing bond with my mom's spirit and knew that she was always there with me, I was inspired to write a heartfelt story for children about a little girl who experiences grief when her mother dies but finds comfort when she learns that her mother is still with her.

I continued attending the annual Conscious Life Expo and had many readings that provided wonderful guidance concerning my life purpose. I was told that I was going to help lots of children and that I was a Lightworker who was working with Archangel Michael to deliver a message. I was also told that Archangel Michael would make my life very difficult but that it would be rewarding. It was the first time I had heard the word, Lightworker, so I started researching what that meant. After reading many descriptions, I felt blessed to be among those who bring healing love and light to humanity by serving others. I knew my book was going to help children who were grieving, but I didn't know I was going to develop such a strong connection with the angels.

In the next few years, I worked diligently to try to self-publish my grief book. I had a grief center interested in working with me, and I had become a certified grief recovery specialist. Everything was in place, but the universe had other plans. After running into continuous roadblocks, I made the heartbreaking decision to set the book aside. You may have heard the saying, 'When one door closes, another one opens.' Well, that's exactly what happened.

During those years when I was working to put the grief book into the marketplace, I was also developing a very powerful relationship with the angels. It started with 'angel numbers,' a method the angels use to communicate, and then moved on to clairaudience or hearing words in my head. One day, to my amazement, I was channeling poetry from the angels! I was given not one but three manuscripts of poetry to help children – to let children know they are never alone and always loved. I was being guided to teach children about angels before focusing on grief.

As I decided to let the angels lead the way, in January of 2014, I put my first channeled manuscript into production, and the project moved forward with effortless synchronicity. Three months later, I became a certified spiritual teacher. Six months after that, I became a certified angel intuitive. On October 27, 2014, Angels, Angels, Everywhere was published. In my dedication, I thanked Archangel Michael for his constant guidance. I was on my way as a Lightworker!

I love being a Lightworker, and I want others to awaken to their Lightworker within, so I created a blog at www.heartofalightworker.com where I write about various spiritual topics. If you think you might be a Lightworker, please read my entry, 'Top 10 Traits of Lightworkers'. If you resonate with my words, answer your calling. The world needs your Divine light now more than ever. You are here to shine your light so others may find their way.

In the enduring words of one of our most prolific Lightworkers, Dr. Wayne Dyer, 'The greatest joy comes from giving and serving. This giving, loving person is the real you.

Let the real you shine bright!'

With love, light, and angel blessings,

Michelle Beber

Michelle Beber

Michelle Beber is an award-winning author and has certifications as a spiritual teacher, angel intuitive, archangel life coach, angel card reader, and grief recovery specialist. She has appeared on local, national, and international radio shows and podcasts, is a member of the Society of Children's Book Writers and Illustrators, and is a member of Toastmasters International.

***Michelle has a strong social media presence on Facebook, Twitter, Pinterest, and Instagram.
There are links to all of her pages on her website,
www.michellebeber.com***

***Her blog,
www.heartofalightworker.com
may be found there as well.***

Journey to the
Centre of my Soul

By Samantha Moir

I have been asked on many occasions, met with curiosity and inquisition, 'What does a being a Lightworker mean to me?' One word – Purpose. Those in the line of passion as I myself follow, have a few things in common when it comes to embracing their gift. Denial and shame when acknowledging their gifts. Continually feeling that every area regarding 'conventional work' doesn't seem to fit. Knowing and trusting situations and their surroundings. I struggled internally for many years with my knowing that I was different.

Unique, but different. I have been considered an old soul or wise beyond my years. I had a gift deep inside of me that was waiting for me to grow and expand. Situations would arise, that would test my faith in my own power and ability. I would deny my knowing... like myself similarly, the universe had a rebellion that would continually push me to face myself and make me step outside my comfort zones.

Synchronicity was everywhere, from phones ringing when I thought of the person, bumping into them not long after.

I must have looked ridiculous pulling the face of disbelief ALL the time. Shocked and bewildered as I stumbled through life feeling like I was insane, rather than a Lightworker. I would have a power knocking on my door with every situation getting louder and louder. It almost felt as though I was being punk'd or on candid camera. Must have been funny to watch me struggle and squirm in my ignorant denial. As this internal subconscious power grew, a whirling sense of momentum began to shift. It was becoming an internal battle of wills. Rationality versus Soul purpose. Until a stand out moment happened, a Lightning bolt moment ... a moment so secretive and divine that only I could hear it.

I said out loud ... 'I am a Psychic. This is who I am from now and so forth.' Was it transcendent upon the world, not really, a self fulfilling light bulb – Absolutely!

After experiencing all different events and adversities in my life I felt that even though the strength and 'coincidental' experiences had played out just as I has seen and imagined, the confirmations where undeniable. These situations made me feel hopeful and forward facing. In every memory, tragedy and challenge a sense of unwavering inner advice would flow through me. An ability to see the silver lining, life lesson and strength that coursed through my veins. I was beginning to learn to trust myself, trust the universal process,trust, that above all I will never be alone in my choices and experiences. I was stepping out into the world the first steps of spiritual journey. I was aligning my Mind Body and Soul.

What does being a Lightworker mean to me? Gratitude. I finally embraced the journey, I finally stopped speaking of myself as a crazy hippy or a whack pot. I found a way to embrace the amazing gifts that I had from both my heart and Soul. It is an amazing experience to grasp the opportunity with both hands and step into my destiny. The adrenal high was surging and gave me the sense of soaring though my feet where planted on the ground.

The only way I can truly describe the feeling is when you arrive somewhere that is the happening. When you're around people who understand you, people who uplift you in your point of view, being in the right place at the right time. Imagine having that feeling 24/7. It is nothing short of miraculous.

I had problems and insecurities of even discussing after the fact, of what I do for a living. I did however cringe and worry at the response that those around me had for a conventional mother of two who has always worked in traditional roles.

I was taking my first steps outside the box of normality and revealing the gifts that I had once been so unprepared to share. I live in a country town so my worry was not being unrealistic or without caution.

The beauty of it was ... I didn't need to explain. I have been radiating at such a high frequency lately the proof was in the pudding.

I have a glow that you acquire when your fate and dreams collide. On your souls journey. Being in that right place at the right time, every time. The journey has not come without challenges, mishaps and worry. There are plenty along the way that have mocked ridiculed and scoffed. Once you reach this level of awareness, you discover the challenges become prevalent in that battle of universal rebellion. You now are being viewed by the wise universe looking back at you like a stumbling toddler trying to find your balance to take your first steps in the world.

You feel taking the leap and admitting to the world and yourself what your purpose is, that what was in your mind was the most ambitious concern and everything else would cosmically fall into place. This is when the tests truly began.

The doors to the universe would unveil and I had divine access to time, love and skill. This was when the monumental, ground breaking and soul shattering challenges would flow like a rapid river, relentless and unforgiving. I can see in hindsight, why this happened, how I had willed it into existence and how it has benefited me in ways I can't even describe. In order for a Lightworker to move in a genuine, honest, non judgemental, loving zone to truly advance all of your key fundamentals have to be boiled down to purity and truth. It sounds confronting, but I was lead to see and evaluate myself in a loving manner for the first time.

What does it mean to me to be a Lightworker? Challenging. To be that of purity to read for clients, I had to have my ego stripped down to the smallest fraction to really understand what the power of thoughts, intention and love have on not only my own life but those I read for and how to perceive their messages properly. The process genuinely need to respected. This wasn't scientific this was spiritual.

The adversities came all at once, money, commitment to the cause, relationship, support, understanding, clients who were stubborn, cynical and closed.

I had to be prepared to progress with my vulnerability, forgiveness from both inner and outer factors. I had all these areas thrown at me all at once. I questioned spirituality in its entirety. I was intimidated and nervous for the first time since committing to my faith. There comes a moment in every Lightworker's experience predominantly at the beginning when you are unclear of boundaries, intention and protection, when you feel amateur around other more experienced Lightworkers, you consider stepping back and mentally smacking yourself for your naive belief that felt so unwaivered before this new journey to my soul. To really be open to myself I had to do a lot of self talk and trust. I know that I was craving complete honesty and transparency and validation.

All of a sudden for the first time in my life I was doubting my ability.

So in came the next challenge to test my doubt. The scariest part of the process of the readings is when you are delivering information to someone with folded arms and a scowl on their face. The kicker to this feeling is to consider going back to how I was previously, working, denial and feeling lost in my own skin was not even option no matter how difficult the challenge. No one is the harsher critic than I on myself, if I could conquer my new founded insecurities I could master any test with ease.

To this date the hardest part of getting to know myself is allowing myself to be raw and honest no matter what my ego responds.

In hindsight, to really be successful (I use this term to reiterate success for a Lightworker as clear, insightful, direct and correct information for clients) you need to truly back yourself.

My confidence leads me to success through the tougher times. I have learnt invaluable lessons about myself and how I cope.

I feel I have honed into the way I work now as reader. I am relatible and real. I have embraced that this how I feel most comfortable not feel I am getting above myself or beyond someone's grasp or put myself under pressure to 'perform' or 'be on point in every situation'. I have finally found my feet and am growing to a whole new height of satisfaction and fulfillment.

To explain it does not do it justice, I urge everyone to strive for that level of happiness.

I have used my adversities and low emotional points to become another way to relate and help others. Soul gratifying, totally! I think that is the key for any Lightworker, trying to distinguish how you read and how it helps both you and your client moving forward. I want to help others in their plight to discover and embrace their gifts. I want to be the friend that picks them out and uses positive reinforcement to guide them through the harder challenges they face as did I. I want to guide and mentor as I know the yearning a Lightworker has for a teacher.

I believe everyone has a gift. What's your Gift?

My number one question that I am asked when I conduct a reading is, 'How did you know your had this gift?' I would like to think that I have been Divinely chosen that I had entered a small elite group of spiritual beings, as I remark to anyone who asked and reading my journey to here it was a self discovery. Sure, I had other Lightworker's explain that I should embrace this gift but ultimately you know and also know when your ready to develop it further. The more people I talk to, the more I learn, the more I value a gift that can be shared. Truth is, we all have a gift. Everyone single one of us ... you included. In my experience and ability to meet so many people in the work I do, I have yet to come across someone who has not had an experience that they can't vividly remember? Sometimes it can be creepy, spooky or just wholesome and heart warming. I bet you as well, have had an experience that you can remember.

I had to educate myself on how to properly protect, cut cords or have the conscious ability to rise above the energy field to leave it there.

As you develop your skills, you then take shape as your own personal energy barometer. I bet you say to yourself, 'Yeah, I know I have something but what? I don't know if I could do it?' It isn't a Divine moment in time, it isn't something you just wake up with in its full capacity. The signs have been there for as far back as you can remember. Have you felt seen or had an experience that references any of these scenarios?

If you can agree with at least one statement, you are already on your way with your gift.

- **Have you entered a room and been able to pinpoint the exact emotions and energy that is in that room?**
- **Have you woke up in the middle of the night with a feeling of someone being near you, family, loved ones or something else?**
- **Have you ever had a dream, premonition, thought or deja vu?**
- **Have you ever seen, heard, smelt, felt something happen but could explain it. Things moving, tastes, or a knowing that occurs that have no explanation?**
- **Have you ever heard voices, whispering, talking?**
- **Do you know a persons emotions just by being in the room with them?**
- **Felt like you could fly, move in your dreams, see colours around people or nature?**
- **Been upset or felt like a presence of loved one was around?**
- **Have you thought or asked a question, for it to be answered with a sign or confirmation?**
- **Ever had a feeling to change your actions at the last minute, to avoid something rather serious happening?**

I suppose there will be people out there that have never had a single experience, but I doubt that. Once you start becoming aware or taking note of these experiences, they will always start to be become more frequent and obvious. There many different types of people and their gifts. The intimidation factor can be overwhelming to embrace it or even to acknowledge it. Once you become aware of your abilities it is very difficult to dull the new found understanding of yourself. Everyone that has these abilities have fine tuned these skills, they have grown and aided their strengths. It requires more development and advancement but it does start out the same ... an inner knowing.

**There are not Psychic tests,
there is no Psychic rule book.
No closed guidelines in
how or when you use them
or define them.**

You can be born with it, you can be someone who stumbles across it later in life, you can be someone who needs more mentoring, reading and direction. So when I ask the question at the beginning of my own readings, it is not only an insight of the future for my clients, but it's my own way to unveil the tricks behind the curtain and initiate everyone to this very inclusive club.

There will always for me and you be moments of
self doubt and worry that you are not hitting the
mark, these are the challenges set to test our faith
in ourselves. I can not promise it will be easy but
like listening to a radio I focus on the beat and the
melodies; everything else is background noise.
The journey is rewarding, gratifying and an
adventure with an outcome bigger than I could,
and still cant even imagine. Being myself is to be
a Lightworker, being a Lightworker is to be myself.
What does it mean to me to be a Lightworker?

Everything.

Samantha Moir

Samantha is a mother of two crazy energetic boys and a slightly crazy partner. She lives in Toowoomba, QLD – a regional city, filled with flowers, festivals and country living. She is an Intuitive Reader, conducting readings and helping to relay messages of guidance. She really enjoys spending time with her kids, exploring the outdoors – from the beach to the rain forest.

Samantha has been writing for herself for as long as she can remember, but since the launch of her business, she has been an advocate of promoting self-awareness and joining others on their own spiritual paths. Samantha enjoys all the essentials in life; a good book, a glass of wine, and flannelette PJs. Passion is her main passion in life. She really enjoys seeing others fulfill their destiny; aiding them find their own passion and integrating them into their lives. You can normally find her having an impromptu dance party in her lounge room with her kids, climbing mountains and dragging her partner along to admire the view, or having a dinner with her girlfriends while laughing into the wee hours of the morning.

You can see more about Sam and her business at www.loveandlight-intuitivereadings.com or find her on Facebook

My Journey (extract from Life is *What Happened*)

By Rosa Carrafa

My first memory of realising that something was 'different' about me was when I was dreaming recurring dreams. This become almost confronting to me as a little girl of about five years old to share with my mother at the time. I do remember I told my dream and then she, my mother gave me a little hug assuring me that it was 'only a dream'. So how does a young child receive answers?

Well, I just learnt that over time I selected the dreams that I wanted to share with others. Not all my dreams were happy, many were mysterious and some were frightening. I later learnt as an adolescent that these were premonitions and messages from God. He, God, speaks through us here on earth to help continue his son Jesus' ways of healing and prophesying. One may say that dreaming is only a fragment of your imagination, however, when I dreamt in the past or dream in the present, I know the difference between a dream of a conscious one and of a subconscious message.

Premonitions via dreaming is one area how I have grown to accept my journey in the spiritual world.

I have experienced a combination. Although many of the dreams or night messages I have are those of a spiritual encounter from a passed loved one, a message to prepare me for what is to come or a message for another. I will share with you a particular spiritual message I had re-occurring as a young girl, this one I did share with my mother as well as many more.

Dream example: I would be lying in bed and I will be able to see myself in the flesh as I would be looking over myself. I would have what I later found out as an out of body experience. This would happen quite often and would also allow me to 'see' the dream I was having too. Was it three or five dimensional?

As a young person you can only imagine how confusing yet comforting it was to experience such 'astral' movements.

Yes, later on as is now, I am able to communicate with the dreams I have and incorporate the messages and experiences with my work in developing each spiritual aspect I have, one at a time, one day at a time through the hope I have inside to keep striving to help others and in turn nurture each aspect.

Growing up in an Italian Catholic – Christian family prepared me for the comforting voices and messages that I continued to receive. I knew that through God I was always safe and looked after, no matter what life challenges came my way. Going to church was not only a ritual within our family, but an absolute vital part of our weekend. Sunday was church day and also the day that the most delicious meal was served at lunch or even dinner if there was an extra special occasion. So now as a young lady of thirteen years old I was beginning to ask many questions about my faith to my mother who was a devout Catholic and read from her little white leather bound bible at church. She was ever so gentle and I now know that she was humouring me as I was asking one question after the other.

> **Till this day, I remember asking her**
> **'does God still love me even**
> **if I can be cheeky and still want**
> **to know why he does things**
> **that he does to us and to the world?'**

Her response was direct as she sensed that I was now all grown up and I was not standing satisfied with short dissatisfied responses. So with this she elaborated on her personal experience as a young girl, how she met my father and her ups and downs with family. This all made sense as she was talking to me and paused every so often with a sigh and then recommenced her sharing with another breath and said to herself something along the line of 'God give me strength as I tell this child of mine about some hard truths about life, family and God'.

> **Well, here I got it, the truth**
> **finally of how things are**
> **the way they are in my family**
> **and why she was so sad when she**
> **was left alone to reflect on her life.**

All the while, through all she was sharing with me, not once did she express any negative word or gesture about God.

Instead, I remember her looking me in the eyes and telling me that 'God sometimes can teach you just like your teacher does and he can also discipline you just like mummy and daddy'.

Okay, so this was beginning to make sense to me as to why some things are the way they are. Immediately, I thought 'how beautiful and innocent' my mother was as she opened her heart to me.

So here I learnt that
yes I am special as I am me.
I am exactly the person
I am supposed to be.

With all the dreams I dreamt that eventually did unfold, I am now officially at ease with myself. Being surrounded with so much love as a child was such a blessing. All those times that I questioned 'WHY is this happening?' were now being answered.

My mother would sit me down while she would be sewing me an outfit and share stories of how she felt as a teenager and meeting our father – her husband. All the unconventional ways and stories of how my father's mother was different as she helped people heal with prayer and how people came to see her from a distance, was shared.

How all that she taught us with the Italian playing cards was actually reading someone's life story through the art in the cards. How as she rubbed her hands on our tummy and touched our foreheads as little children as she prayed then dipped oil to water was her way of connecting with God and his works through us.

Our grandmother was a remarkable woman she not only made sure we called her 'mamma', which is the respectful and traditional Italian way of referring a woman of her stature as the matriarch in our family.

So here began the interesting story of how I was named after her and how I will probably be like her. If I am somewhat like her in anyway, then I am privileged.

To those who have an opinion of this, let it be known that I no longer am holding back on my spirituality and my belief system. I respect you for who you are. If you for some reason find it questioning to my faith or 'how' I choose to help others, lead my life and the life choices I have made along the way, then I can only share with you that you are free to live, think, speak and act as you so please.

Only remember that we each have a story and as you have yours, I have mine.

With this, I send you peace and love.

Rosa Carrafa
My journey called life is not that different from yours. Names, places and culture are mostly the things that may alter.

My passion in life is going through every goal I set and making them a reality.

As an artist and Devotional Faith guide, a published author and a woman who will continue to reach out to as many people as I can with messages that may influence their lives on a more profound and eternal level. With each goal I fulfill, I move on to the next. All of which none of these would have been possible without the love that surrounds me and my faith that keeps me striving with hope to look forward to tomorrow.

*As a Devotional Faith guide, I learn through you and our time together.
As a mother, I learn from my children.
As a woman, I learn from other women around me in the present and the past.
As a person, I learn from my surroundings that the earth naturally gifts me.
As your sister, I learn from your pain.
As your friend, I learn from your life experiences and those that you share with me.*

As an orphan child and now adult, I learn that grief never really goes away and that those we lose via death is a valuable lesson to us to live each day and give gratitude for each moment we experience.

These moments, regardless if they be great or not so great, make me, you and everyone who walks this earth special as we each have a vital role to play in this somewhat theatrical journey called life.

Released in 2016:
'Aspects of Me' – an affirmation book aimed at inspiring children, teens and adults alike to live a confident and empowered life.

Upcoming projects:
'Aspects of Heaven' – a peaceful journey with loss, faith, grief and hope.
'Where art comes to life' – Unique art and devotional messages.

Author's page:
https://www.facebook.com/RosaCarrafaAuthorArtist
Devotional faith page:
https://www.facebook.com/SpiritualAspects
Blog:
http://ourspiritualaspects.blogspot.com.au

Sophialina's
Experience

By Sophialina Baldock

Lightworker to me is a soul that has made an agreement before birth to come here to earth to teach, heal, hold space and wayshow through acts of self-love and knowledge. They feel things on a very deep level and quite often feel outcast or different from others. When they go out, they transmute and clear old paradigms and spaces as they go along. This takes a lot of energy sometimes and can make them tired.
For this reason, most Lightworkers often prefer to be alone to keep the energies around them calm.

I'd like to introduce myself, my name is Sophialina. I first found out I was a Lightworker in 2015. I had no idea what the term was and decided to look into it. I've always felt different on a deeper level and that my purpose was special, but what was it exactly? It was a passing thought here and there throughout my life, not knowing it was my Guides. I would question things and in some form that lead me to teaching and healing. No matter how much I fought it, these feelings would keep coming up. So I decided to surrender and began to allow no matter what. In this lifetime I feel my purpose is to guide, teach, and facilitate healing through living and being a true Wayshower.

On my journey so far I've come up against many things on my path. Things I had to heal or feel so I could shift energy. To name a few bullying, abuse, and some very interesting experiences with mentors.

> **When I think back to how I overcame many of my sufferings and healed them, it all came back to self-love and showing myself forgiveness and compassion in my daily life.**

I diligently spoke affirmations, cleared my aura and meditated. This all helped however, there were some key elements I was missing. This was when I started to look into healing modalities that stood out to me.

Slowly I shifted away from being a shy, insecure, powerless person to stronger and more confident. I placed effort and self-worth into my daily practice. I found blogging and creating videos also helped me bit by bit. I found the more I stepped out of my comfort zone, the more I would expand and make a contribution to the collective.

> **When we are on our journey we must stay true to ourselves, our truth and divinity.**

When I found out that I was a Lightworker I fell into this state of looking outside myself. I latched on to a community that came across my path and became so engrossed that I became lost. My purpose, my light was not even me anymore it was as if I was a stranger. My identity was gone at this time I couldn't even think, feel or decide what Sophialina's truth was anymore. What I would like to say and guide others to do if you find yourself in this same situation is to seek out your own truth with your innate within you. Shift into your heart space and honor it. This is imperative, it almost has taken me two months of clearing out beliefs that were not mine to get to a place where I can talk about this part of my journey. I would cry many times when I couldn't fulfill what I was asked do. My life away from this became very out of balance and like any instrument we must tune-up ourselves. I woke up and I absolutely learned some valuable tools from this situation. One thing I learned was the higher I vibrated and shined my light the less I would need to protect my light. The stronger I would feel energetically. You see as Lightworkers we are here to transform the darkness not hide from it. Which is something that was a double standard in this community. So if we go out let's shine, heal and be the light houses we are meant to be.

I found with taking the courses I mention above, it seemed easier to say I was a Holistic Intuitive Healer. I find myself being super curious of many modalities because like a puzzle, they are all pieces that begin to fit.

**Being gifted in many ways
my main loves are Sacred Geometry
and Channeling symbols.
Channeling has become a
beautiful outlet for me to
receive information,
and work with an aspect of myself
that is from the star system Pleiades.**

The Pleiades are just one of many Starseeds that we may have been. Starseeds can be described as souls who have lived in other planetary systems as well as on Earth. I used to deny that I was a Starseed because there was not a lot of information available at the time that wasn't linked to fear. Faces would appear in windows as would spirits. I was terrified and never said a word because I felt no one would believe me. Other modalities

I perform are Reiki, Past Life Regressions, Theta Healing®, Akashic Record and of course Intuitive Readings.

At this time I don't follow any religious organisations, I follow my inner Creator inside. I feel we create our own reality through the thoughts, words and actions we send out. I believe in going within and not seeking outside ourselves for information or truth.

If I can share any wisdom to anyone it would be: trust the feelings you receive, know that all words and actions carry a vibration, and they are unique to each individual.

Look past flaws and see the person in their core energy. It is there that we see the Creator collective. If we can begin to shift our reactions, we can shift the collective consciousness toward unity.

I would like to end with one of my favorite quotes from one of the only Mentors that I resonated with for most of my journey.

'Spirituality must be lived not just studied. All the books in the world will not help us if we do not live what we learn.'

Kryon

Sophialina Baldock
Sophialina is an intuitive healing facilitator and Master Lightworker. She is native to Canada and has been o n her path for almost 20 years.

She truly enjoys and loves mentoring and teaching others. She also loves to volunteer locally with non-profit business.

Much love.

Facebook:
www.facebook.com/IntuitiveSpiritRegeneration
Instagram:
www.instagram.com/sophialina11/?hl=en
Twitter:
www.twitter.com/SophialinaB

*© **Sophialina Baldock 2016***

The Pathway of the Soul
A Journey from Darkness into Light

By Matthew Halligan

My journey as a Lightworker began on 23rd February 1953 (7), the day of my birth, and entry into the physical plane. My journey carried me through the depths of addiction and alcoholism, isolation, rejection, depression, and eventually into the prevailing light. My resident and core fear of abandonment which I ultimately had to face and experience was, I believe designed so that I could come to the understanding by way of awareness and life experiences that I could never be abandoned, as I was an integral part of a 'whole' called Universal Intelligence or the Creator.

I was born the seventh child in a family of eight children. My birth number and position of birth in the family had significant meaning for me during my life. As I became aware of number seven in my life and it's repetitive appearance at times of change or significant events I began to wonder just what it was and what was meant by this biblical and divine number and its presence in my life. My life story and search for meaning and purpose had begun.

As I became more aware of the presence of number seven in my life, I began to look closely at significant events and when they had occurred.

As mentioned earlier, I was born on the 23rd day of February 1953 (7). My father was born in 1910, which meant he was 43 years of age when I was born. I was the seventh child in the family. My first taste of alcohol was at age 16 years, a taste which would not go away until I was 41 years of age, 25 years later! The number of our house was number seven and my father passed in his 70th year.

I journeyed the Camino, a pilgrimage to Santiago De Compostella in July 1996, only to recognise that the celebration date of 25th July was in fact the feast day of the Saint. I learned about the Essenes, a separatist sect who lived in Qumran on the shores of the Dead Sea and authors of the Dead Sea Scrolls. I learnt of their communion with the angels of the Earth during the day and the angels of the heavens in the evening, seven days per week. I traveled to Jerusalem to visit their place of origin, and I experienced separation and divorce as part of my journey through alcoholism and recovery. I remarried on the 29th July 2005 (7) and have a daughter who was born in the 7th year of our relationship. My new partner had two children from a previous marriage, I had four children from my first marriage. My daughter Alexandra was the seventh child from both relationships. In 1994 I experienced 43 nights in an addiction treatment centre, and the room given to me? Yes, you've guessed it ... room number seven.

I began to realise and believe that I had been given a gift from the universe, a gift in the form of a number which would act as a compass and guide assisting me in my life's journey.

A number/sign which would offer me comfort at times when I was doubtful and uncertain. This sign was a gift to me from the universe to help me realise that I would always be given a sign that 'everything is as it should be' and that the universe was always working with me for my highest good. I had my own universally driven global positioning system straight from the eternal heavens. All I had to do was trust and that my friend, took a lot of patience and practice as it meant surrendering to the unknown. It was a journey which I had to participate in, and the pathway would be guided and signposted by numeral 7 to a destination which was unknown to me.

> **My mission as a Lightworker included experiences of loneliness, depression, apathy, mistrust, confusion and how I, as an emissary of light was going to assist other human beings in achieving their individual life's purpose.**

I would be woken at 3am with an endless download of spiritual information, which I would note in my well worn out notepads only to experience a lack of enthusiasm and motivation with how I was to share this wisdom and information with my fellow human beings. At times I felt angry and dismayed because if I was chosen to be an emissary of light, what was the purpose of giving me all this information and not being able to share it with my fellow humans? Deep in my psyche I had a constant niggle about a book. If I could not share this wisdom with people at seminars and presentations, was it to be done by way of a book? Where was I to start? What was it's title, and how was I meant to compile and index all of this information for the ultimate birth of my book in the material plane?

I began to symbolise my book as a pregnancy and birth; a similar process to that of humans and other species on the planet. Firstly, there is potential to create something.

Then, the fusion of both masculine and feminine energy. After that comes a gestation period, and finally, the birth in the material realm. So, how was the idea of my book relative to the four stages of my creative process?

The potential is, that all the information is available to us in the higher realms. What I needed was the fusion of both masculine and feminine energies.

I began to realise that my intuition and knowing was, in fact, my feminine side which would relay the required information to me, and that my masculine side would have to take the action and begin recording the downloads.

The big question for me then was, did I trust myself, and the process? That was the real test. To believe in my conviction, in my intuition and more importantly, to believe in myself and the role I had been given as a Lightworker.

Before the book could begin in earnest I experienced random and impulsive writing on different mediums over a period of time. I was unable to find the 'right location' and the 'right method' of writing which suited me. I was trying to structure my writing in an organised way, where in actual fact the writing and downloads were random and unstructured by nature. Once I accepted this fact, I was free to write anything which was downloaded to me and leave it to someone else to edit the randomness, while placing structure on the writing. I began to experience the freedom of writing in my own natural and free flowing way. Phew! What a relief!

I am also a talented photographer, who is always aware of the changing light in my surroundings – a light which varies with intensity and reflection, depending on the subject on which it falls and is reflected back. My photography was the first step in my love and awareness of the existence of light, and the stark contrast between its presence and its absence from subject to subject. I began to wonder whether it could be the same, or similar for people like me who had experienced addiction. With the absence of light and the presence of darkness, they disconnect from their spiritual or a light-being and connect with the non-spiritual or darker side of material life. I began to wonder whether our journey through life was actually one from darkness into light, and a return or reconnection with our true light and spiritual essence. After all, don't we experience going from darkness into light each evening and into the new morning, and don't seeds when planted begin their journey from the darkness of the soil and ascend towards the light of the sun?

In this light (if you pardon the pun), was addiction a separation from my divine self?

A journey into the darkness which would ultimately lead me on a journey of reunification with my divine self and into the light. A journey of reconnection and reunification with my divine being.

From darkness into light, a journey of reunification with the true light and higher self.

I experienced this in a symbolic way in the early days of my treatment for alcoholism. One night in the addiction treatment centre while reading a book in my bed, I became aware of a light outside of my bedroom door. This light seemed to be shining through the keyhole and doorframe. I knew instinctively that I had to invite this light into me. So I placed the book on the bed, lay there with my palms facing upwards and invited the light into me.

It was then that I experienced and felt what I can only describe as a strong electric shock in my solar plexus and navel area; a shock which pinned me to the bed. As I lay there in both delight and confusion, I realised I had connected with my source; one which I was disconnected from during my 25 years of active addiction to alcohol. It was then that I began my journey back to my source, and I was consciously aware of light as a guiding factor in my life. As with all things that return to their source;

my body to the Earth, the rivers to the sea, the sea to the ocean, did I. I too, was on a journey; a return journey to my source via the divine light of my Creator.

'From the source I came, and to the source, I shall return.'

My addiction years eventually lead me to become a qualified addiction counsellor and life coach. My creative side as I now know to be my creative feminine energy, assisted me with the creation of centres for people who felt and had been marginalised and isolated within the community because of their addiction and associated behaviours.

I spent many constructive and positive years working with people like myself who had been lost and by various life experiences had been placed on a journey of self-discovery and recovery.

I wondered had they been placed on my path, or had I been placed on theirs? Either way, we had something to learn from and about each other.

My experience of addiction was a place I did not want to be, however, it was also a place I did not want to leave. But, how was I to ascend and reach my purpose and meaning if I remained stuck in the darkness of addiction? There is a big possibility that I would have died, just like the seed which did not germinate it would rot and die in its dark and lonely place in the Earth. I began to realise that change was assisted by an accommodating factor; an outside force which facilitated personal change at the right moment in time.

I became aware of my resistance to change and what it was that kept me anchored in a place I wanted to leave, but feared to leave.

I believed that I wouldn't be able to manage on my own; I feared abandonment and rejection. All of these fears were my resistors to change and had me anchored to the harbour wall so that my sail could not kiss the wind and travel to a new port of call on my journey. I was stuck, and resisting change because of the fear of what would happen to me.

I did not (at that time) see or believe that the universal mind was actually offering me a life experience that was giving me the opportunity for transition and change, in order to embrace my journey of ascension and soul awakening.

> **Today, I see things in a different light and embrace and accept change much easier in the knowledge that the universe is working with me for my development and not against me.**

I now recognise that the universe was offering me a pathway by which I could ascend, but first, I had to change my perception.

You see, recovery and sobriety – especially the latter – is not altogether about the absence of alcohol or the drug of choice. It's about the presence of those things which can contribute to the person's well-being. It's a measure of polarity. For example, we know about good and bad, up and down, wet and dry, hot and cold. Each one, including sobriety and addiction is relative; relative to the amount of what is and what is not present at any given time. Darkness is relative to the amount of light which is available at any given time. Dryness is relative to the amount of moisture present at any given time, and so forth.

As I live near the sea, I am conscious of the daily tides and the rhythm. The difference between high and low tide is obviously the amount of water present at any given time depending on the orbit of the Moon, and the cycle is relative to the frequency of the tides each day.

Wouldn't it be wonderful if I could assist people with identifying the frequencies and cycles in their own lives so that they could break free from their self imposed prisons?

I became aware that our ability to change is facilitated by external experiences and internal motivation. We have our own personal internal combustion engine which is fueled by our emotions. These emotions facilitate change which is assisted by a spark. This spark is the accommodating factor represented by the experience. Change was, and still is happening all around us. I can't help but notice and watch the Earth as she unfolds by way of the elemental factors of Fire, Water, Air, and Earth. I notice on TV, whenever there is flooding in one part of the world, there are fires elsewhere, coupled with the odd earthquake and hurricane which are not far behind.

Mother Earth is constantly changing and reshaping herself into something new, while her essence remains the same.

Should the principles of 'as above so below' be correct, Mother Earth, is in this case, on her own spiritual journey of Ascension just like us humans and everything else residing on planet Earth. With this principle of change in mind, I created, developed and structured a system for embracing change.

It's called 'The Livingwheel System for Managing Change' and is designed to promote balance and realignment in the person's life which in turn, creates a sense of wellness and connectedness.

I believe I've been given this gift to assist people accommodate change, which will assist them to restore balance and realignment in their lives.

This reunification with self and is what is required by people to reconnect with their mission, and help them remember what they have forgotten; that they have a mission and are connected to all things. In having gained this awareness and by accepting it, it helps them on their journey as they ascend to a higher vibrational awareness via the experience been presented to them at any given time. Each new experience, therefore, becomes an opportunity for growth and spiritual awareness. I am of the belief that the universe is working with us and assisting us on our journey of ascension.

The Livingwheel System for Managing Change recognises that we are all connected. The Livingwheel is a nine stage model of engaging and interacting with personal life issues. It offers a systemic approach, while recognising that we live a life of choices; choices based on the experience presented to us at any given time. It assists the person uncover, discover and recover from old, self-defeating negative patterns of behaviour by raising personal awareness of the reasons why they choose to engage with or resist the process of change. Simplified, its an introspective tool of creation with the understanding that from the destruction of old thinking and behaviours, comes the creation of newness. This system was created to facilitate change and assist with the restoration of balance and harmony into people's troubled lives.

> **I think as a Lightworker,
> I've been chosen by the Creator
> to shine light on reality by way
> of sharing wisdom and information
> given to me via my spiritual 'downloads'.**

I believe my intuition is my soul's way of communicating with me in its own unique, quiet and gentle way. I feel my soul (my feminine side or feminine energy) is in direct contact with the greater unconscious or universal mind and that it's up to me (my masculine side or masculine energy) to take action and to trust the information given to me. I'm now in the process of cognitive co-creation where I'm creating as an emissary of light on behalf of the Creator, with the purpose of assisting humanity on their journey of ascension.

The frustration and anxiety that I feel at this time are severe, as although I'm aware of my gift and my direct contact with divine wisdom, I have no outlet to share this information with. I often find myself questioning and having doubts as to my belief in my intuition. I find myself asking, 'What use is all of this information? Why have I been chosen to share this information, when I have no outlet or venue to share this wonderful gift with others?' It's then that I dig deep again and try to have faith that this is all happening for a purpose.

Similar to being on a journey and not knowing the destination, but having faith that I am on the right road; that my gift of communication and intuition work together and perhaps the way to share this information is by writing, taking the form of a book. That way I'm sharing my gift with all of humanity and on my return to the light I will have contributed to the growth and ascension of all concerned and it will be recorded in the halls and libraries of the nations.

I will have fulfilled my mission by bringing enlightenment to humanity, given to me by the universe as an emissary of light. This is my belief and I must keep reminding myself of this so as not to become too paralysed with despair and frustration. It's akin to having this wonderful gift; the knowledge with no one to share it with, but I must believe that I am part of a plan and that while I am small, I am significant and an integral part of a greater whole. I must keep repeating my mantra which is, 'The universe at this moment in time, is orchestrating itself in a harmonious way for the best possible outcome in every situation for me.' I must keep believing this and trust that I am part of a process, and like all other processes, they tend to take time from fertilisation to birth.

I will keep reminding myself that I am constantly in a process of becoming; becoming something else. I am constantly evolving, constantly changing and nothing remains the same. Therefore, my current situation will change and become something else, just like me. I will continue to have faith and trust in the process.

I have experienced a journey from darkness into light.

I have traveled from the depths of alcoholism and alcohol addiction into the light of recovery. I have come into realignment, balance, and harmony in my own life. My most rewarding moments are when I sit with people in the darkness of addiction, experiencing fear and despair, and I can shine my light of sobriety and recovery on them without them even knowing.

Since beginning the journey of writing this submission, I have become separated once more. My marriage has reached its end, it has completed it's cycle, and I recognise that I have been redirected; not rejected. Once again I have been given the time and space to link into my mission and perhaps focus more on allowing myself to be directed and guided. I'm now free to express myself to those who can hear and understand what it is I have to say. I must believe that the universe at this moment in time is orchestrating itself in a harmonious way for the best possible outcome for me; its cosmic child, Matthew!

I'm so grateful to the universe and its guiding hand for assisting me on my journey and for helping me understand what I believe to have happened for me. The years of alcoholism were not the best years of my life, however now as I look back and reflect on my years of darkness and my resulting 22 years of light, I appreciate and I'm extremely grateful for the 'gift' of alcoholism which has guided me back on my journey into recovery and back into the light and re-reunification with my Soul.

Namasté Matthew

Matthew Halligan

Writing about other topics; especially those of a spiritual nature, I find much easier than writing about myself. However, here goes! My name is Matthew, which contains 7 letters. I am the 7th child in a family of eight children. My birthdate is the 23rd day of February 1953 (7). My father whose name was also Matthew, was 43 years of age (7) when I was born. I experienced alcoholism and addiction in a cycle of 25 years (7). I spent 43 nights (7) in a therapeutic treatment centre for addiction. I am now, many days in recovery, enjoying sobriety and a new life, days for which I am very grateful. I came to the belief that my addiction was a spiritual disease, which I was treating with chemicals and alcohol.

I have married twice and my daughter Alexandra is 17 years of age. I also have four sons. Alexandra was born in the 7th year of my relationship with her mother and was born prematurely in the 34th week of pregnancy (7). She is the 7th child from both marriages and her full name when calculated adds to 115 (7). I am currently a single parent and live with my daughter and dog Molly, beside the Atlantic Ocean in County Donegal, which is located at the Northwestern tip of Ireland. I believe numeral 7 has been given to me as my personal guide or global positioning system in this life.

It guides me, I believe in its significance and symbolism, and that it acts as a signpost to and for me, with which to follow on my journey of ascension and return to my source. I am a qualified addiction counsellor and spiritual life coach, assisting people in recovery from the darkness of addiction and the fear of embracing life changes, into the light of recovery experiencing a new life of light and hope. My life experiences have awoken me to communication. This entails raising awareness in people of where to look in their lives but not what to see, so that change and balance can re-enter their lives at their pace and time. I believe 'It's not what we experience, it's how we interpret the experience.'

I am now in the process of writing my second book, 'The Pathway Of The Soul – A Journey from Darkness into Light'. My intention is for my book to be published later in 2017.

So, until we meet again as words between the pages, wherever there is darkness in your fellow souls, shine your light, and wherever there is conflict, share your peace. Namasté, Matthew

https://www.facebook.com/livingwheel
http://www.livingwheelcoaching.com

The Journey
to Believe

By Kerrie Bernhard

Once upon a time I didn't believe in much at all. I certainly didn't believe in God or a higher power. Whenever people spoke to me about God I'd say 'Well if God made the universe and everything in it, who made God?' Nobody could give me an answer of course so that was enough doubt for me to not believe. Although I always have been independent and stubborn, and prefer to find things out for myself!

As I approached my late teenage years things began to change and I discovered another side of life – spirituality. I learned how to read tarot cards, I studied numerology and I did a short course in palmistry. I also started reading different books about spiritual topics. I'd like to say that life opened up for me at that point and everything completely changed but it didn't, well not in a profound way. But eventually it would and is ultimately what saved me many times over.

I got into my first relationship at the age of 18 and was engaged at 19. It was a relatively short-lived relationship at two years as it turned out to be physically, emotionally and verbally abusive.

> **I look back now and wonder
> how I ever survived that
> time in my life and why I put up
> with what I did but I don't have
> any clear answer other than
> it was a necessary part of my journey.**

As fate would have it someone witnessed the abuse one day and the relationship ended. I thought I was free, however the next relationship I entered into was also abusive, well for the first year anyway.

After that I made the decision that I had enough and deserved better, and the abuse stopped. We continued the relationship for another six years until our paths took us in different directions.

The damage done in both those relationships would take more than 20 years to undo. And truth be told I'm not sure it ever truly goes away. The shame, the embarrassment, the guilt and the insecurity always live within the shadows of my deepest self, popping up every now and then demanding attention and to be dealt with.

At the age of 21, and early into my second relationship, I attempted suicide. I'm not sure I truly wanted to die but I guess it was my way of saying I had enough. I took an overdose of whatever pills I could find in the house and drank two bottles of Spumante wine. An ambulance was called for me later that night by a friend but when it arrived I pretended that no-one was home until they left. It took almost a week of not being able to eat and throwing up bile before I finally went to see a doctor. I was admitted straight to hospital and found myself in intensive care and on suicide watch. It was a horrible week in hospital and I was extremely close to needing a liver transplant. I had psychologists come to speak to me but in a large room with only curtains as privacy, and a bunch of students sitting in on the sessions, I found myself not having much to say. I often wonder how different my life may have been if I had taken that opportunity to get the help I needed and wanted. But it wasn't to be; my time would come later.

Somewhere around the age of 28 or 29 I entered into my first same sex relationship. It took me by surprise and I guess those who knew me too. Thankfully my family always have and always will support me in my decisions and it was accepted without question, well at least to me anyway. It was still a very confusing and confronting time in my life as I really didn't like to be labelled. I didn't want to be gay, a lesbian or bisexual. I just wanted to be me.

My next relationship was also with a female and this would be one of the most defining of my life, for all the wrong and eventually right reasons. There were lots of good times in our five years together but I hadn't dealt with my sexuality at the stage when we first connected and I wasn't ready for another serious relationship. Unfortunately by the time I sorted through my issues and realised that she was the one for me we had already broken up and she had met someone else. We reconciled shortly after that but she ended up cheating on me with the person she had met, just before we were due to move in together. It completely shook my world.

> **I had opened up my heart fully for the first time in my life and it got crushed beyond anything I thought possible.**

At that point I had a breakdown. I couldn't function properly and I found myself crying all the time, even at work. I remember coming home one day and lying on the floor curled up in the foetal position near my front door and sobbing like a crazy person. The betrayal was painful but to be honest I think it was a combination of all that I had held in for so many years that was finally ready to be acknowledged and released. That was breaking point for me and thankfully someone I worked with saw the pain I was in and organised for me to have a counselling session. That was the beginning of my journey back to me.

I look back now and take responsibility for my part in all the relationships and the wrong doings in my life. It does takes two to tango as they say and whilst I may not have been the person to dish out the abusive, the lies, the betrayal or the hurt I was the person accepting it and I was the common denominator in them all.

> **I forgave my partner for cheating and we stayed together for another three years but the damage done could never truly be repaired.**

At the end of the relationship I swore I'd never enter another one until I was in the right place within myself to attract the right person and spent eight years (which felt like a blink of an eye really) being single. Strangely enough though, as life sometimes is, I reconnected my ex very briefly after being single for seven years. Whilst it turned out to be another painful experience, it was a blessing in disguise as I was able to fully let go of the past and we salvaged a friendship from the wreckage.

Somewhere around the age of 28 my dad (who was only in his forties at the time) had a major stroke. He spent a couple of weeks in intensive care and had to have part of his brain removed. He lost movement down one side of his body and while he miraculously kept his long term memory he was never the same again.

> **My father survived the stroke but the dad I had always known died that day and I still mourn the loss of that at times.**

It was such a defining moment for my family and I have no doubt that many of the tragedies and disappointments that have occurred since then, within my immediate family, would not have happened if dad had not had that stroke.

> **Then unexpectedly, at the age of 36,
> I found out that my father
> was not in fact
> my biological father.**

It was a shock to say the least but in some strange way it also felt like a missing piece of puzzle clicked in to place. It took some dealing with but in the end it hasn't affected the relationships I have with my family. I don't think about it all that often now but in the back of my mind I sometimes wonder who my biological family are and where they might be.

But amongst all that has happened to me in life, what I have detailed really is just the tip of the iceberg. They are all significant moments, along with the sexual abuse I experienced from a family member as a child.

> **But the beauty of my story
> is that not one of these moments
> ever truly broke or defined me.
> Each one has been a
> valuable lesson for my soul
> and has been a vital part
> of my journey in this human
> incarnation as a Lightworker.**

Everything that I have experienced has given me insight and understanding to help myself and to help others.

Without any of it I wouldn't be who I am and that would change everything.

**It is ironic how once upon a time
I never believed in much at all
yet believe has always been the
one word that has stuck with me
and has been what I consider my mantra.**

I had an intuitive piece of art commissioned back in 2011 with the word believe and that is what truly triggered this journey to believe (on a professional level) and to help others to believe. I will always be grateful to the beautiful soul who gave me the gentle push, inspiration and encouragement I needed.

At the end of 2012 after 15 years of working within community services in local government I left my full-time job. I knew I had more to offer the world than what I was doing behind a desk, and after never truly having a clear direction in my life of what I wanted to do I discovered life coaching. It was perfect for me because it focuses less on problems and more on solutions.

**It's about helping people
get from where they are
to where they want to be.**

As much as our past shapes who we are, I do believe that it never needs to define us. I started my own coaching and consulting business in 2013 and have been doing this ever since.

But it was 2016 that was a truly defining year for me. In one of those lightbulb moments I had a realisation early in the year.

**That there is nothing I need
to change about myself to be
any more worthy of having what I desire.**

In fact there is nothing anyone needs to change about themselves to be any more worthy of having what they desire. I don't have to change my looks, my body, my income, my environment, anything at all, to be any more worthy. That realisation has been a life changing revelation for me.

At the beginning of that year I also set a word for myself, a theme for my year if you like, and the word was alignment.

Not surprisingly my life aligned beautifully in so many ways. I love how the universe works! The words 'the more you believe the more you achieve' came to me in a moment of inspiration and from there Kerrie Lee Intuitive Belief Coach was born. I got clarity and direction for my work, developed a new logo and branding, and combined my spiritual and practical knowledge and skills to help people believe in themselves, in life, in love and in spirit.

As a Lightworker I support, guide and inspire people to believe and make positive change in their lives.

Through intuitive coaching, card readings, programs and handcrafted inspirational products, I am able to use my life experiences to help others. I also give a lot of my time and energy to providing free daily and weekly readings on social media, and engaging with my followers in meaningful ways. Knowing that I can, and do, make a difference in this world makes all of my life experiences, both positive and negative, worthwhile.

2016 also saw a long held and cherished dream of mine become a reality; I had my first book published. It began with a dream about the words 'from ordinary to extraordinary' and almost unbelievably, within weeks of the dream I was signing a book publishing deal with White Light Publishing House to write my very first book '111 Beliefs to transform your life from ordinary to extraordinary'! It was all so divinely guided and inspired by the angels and I still pinch myself to make sure it's real. It is; I'm a published author!!

And not to be outdone the universe had one other special treat in store for me; love. I never gave up on believing in great and true love and I am so pleased to share that I have a wonderful man in my life who loves me unconditionally. The angels saw fit to bring us together in a beautiful way after 12 months of a purely platonic relationship. Unexpected for us both but it just goes to show that when the time is right what is meant to be will be.

I truly believe this is just the beginning of another wonderful part of my life journey, on both a professional and personal level. Having celebrated my 44th birthday I am excited for the journey ahead! Anything truly is possible when you believe. I am what I would call a very ordinary person (in an extraordinary way, as we all are) and if I can have my dreams come true from simply believing in myself, in life, in love and in spirit, you can too.

So remember...the more you believe the more you achieve!!

Kerrie Bernhard
I coach. I inspire. I support. I create.
I write. I dream. I believe.

My name is Kerrie Lee and I am an intuitive belief coach, certified angel card reader and author. I am passionate about making the world a better place and believe that starts with each one of us as individuals. With the help of the angels I support and guide people to believe in themselves, in life, in love and in spirit so that they can live the life their heart is calling to them. I combine my practical and spiritual knowledge, skills and experience to provide the tools people need to believe and create long-lasting and positive change in their life.

You can find Kerrie on Facebook:
www.facebook.com/kerrieleebeliefcoach

Now, I Understand

By Christie Lyons

I've only recently acknowledged that I am a Lightworker, and when I say recently, I mean in the last few years. Subconsciously of course, I have always known this about myself, but could never quite pinpoint why I felt the way I did, or why I had to experience certain things throughout my life before I could reach this understanding. But now, I understand.

Every single thing that I have experienced in this lifetime so far makes absolute sense – from becoming ill whenever there were lots of people around me as a young child, never really 'fitting in' in high school, to all of the heartbreaking challenges I'd been through in such a short period of time. At the time of course, I was confused, felt isolated, and didn't know what this longing was inside of me that I wasn't able to fulfil no matter how hard I tried. It was as if a piece of me was yet to be unearthed; that there was a part of me that was going to be triggered at some point in time; I just didn't know when or what it was. I knew that I was here in this lifetime for a very important purpose, but it took me a long time to figure out what that was.

But now, I understand, and now, I know what that purpose is. In fact, I can sum all of it up in a much better way:

> **I now know who I am.**
> **I am a Lightworker**
> **– always have been –**
> **I just had to figure it out**
> **in my own time.**

There are many significant moments in my life that assisted me on my journey to awakening, but a few in particular stand out to me as being the sparks that ignited this light within me, allowing me to delve deeper into myself and my purpose; helping me to understand who I really was and how every single moment of my life up until then resembled pieces of a puzzle that I was finally beginning to piece together. Each of those moments that pushed me to really go within were in relation to my children.

My eldest child, who is now a teenager, arrived into this world more than five weeks premature and is not only my son, but a kindhearted, sensitive soul who continues to amaze me every single day with how resilient and compassionate he is. His life has been turned upside down, inside out, and every which way in between, and to put it briefly, he has experienced being the victim of bullying, emotional abuse, and upheaval over the years, which has seen him depressed, suffering anxiety, and struggling at times to understand where he belongs and who he is.

In spite of his challenges however, he stands firm in being the empathetic and compassionate young man that he is, and because of what he has experienced, now uses his wisdom to help his peers who are in a dark place or need support. I have no doubt in my mind that he chose me to be his Mum because he knew when we signed up for this life together, that I would never judge him, never condemn him for being sensitive; but encourage him to embrace who he is wholly and proudly. And now, he is doing just that. My son is a beautiful, kind soul, who is already helping to heal the world, and through overcoming his challenges, is also an assertive young man whose strength astounds me. My eldest son teaches me every day – he likely doesn't know it – but he does. He teaches me that I, too, can be as resilient as he is, and can turn my challenges into strength and wisdom to help others. For this, my beautiful son, I thank you.

> **In late 2012, I miscarried.
> This child I was carrying
> inside of me had decided
> to return Home,
> and I was heartbroken
> and so, so confused.**

This precious child decided that she wasn't ready to enter the world just yet, and this had me questioning absolutely everything about life itself. I read articles and books, joined forums and groups on the internet, and sat in silence, crying my heart out for some time. It wasn't until I read a life–changing book written by my (now) dear friend, Karen, that the pieces started coming together, and I was able to understand this experience fully.

> **This heartbreaking occurrence
> pushed me to go within and
> find the answers, and once I did,
> I expressed them on paper.**

The past hurts (not just this one – but all of them) bled onto the pages, mixed with tears, anger and sadness, but the moment the words were written, I could physically feel them being released. I have held onto so much negativity and pain over the years, and I didn't even realise it. Losing this child momentarily was something that needed to occur in order for me to heal, and not only did I begin to heal, but all that releasing allowed room for me to find myself again; the person I hadn't even realised until then that I'd lost. This is where my spiritual awakening really began.

Less than twelve months later, I gave birth to my little Heart Warrior. This treasured little man was born prematurely, just like his older brother, but little did we know at the time of his birth, that he would be faced with a challenge that I still, to this day, am amazed that he was able to overcome.

I still remember the moment I walked into the special care nursery at the hospital; just arriving to visit my little man as I had already been sent home, and he had to remain there as he was not able to feed just yet. I walked into the ward to see the empty humidicrib and my heart raced. A nurse came to speak with me right away and asked me to follow her into another room, where I saw six or seven doctors and specialists huddled around my baby boy.

I was told in so many words that my little man was drowning in his own blood and that he was being transferred to the Children's Hospital.

At that moment, I had no idea what to do or how to feel. Was he going to die?

As the nurses and paramedics prepared him for the short trip to the children's hospital, I did the only thing I could do – I reached into the small hole in his humidicrib and held his tiny little hand. I just watched him and cried. I couldn't even hold him and it tore me apart. It was at that moment that I received a message from one of my Lightworker friends, explaining to me how to send healing energy to his heart. It's interesting that in those desperate moments – the ones where you feel you simply must believe and have faith, how powerful it can be. So, I did it. I squeezed my left arm through the hole, placed my palm over my little boy's heart, and envisioned Archangel Raphael's emerald green light shining through my heart, out of my hand, and into his tiny, broken heart.

> **I had never felt anything like it before in my life, and I could feel this beautiful healing light flowing through my body and into his.**

I sobbed, and my own heart was breaking, but I felt it. Not only did I feel the strength being given to my little boy, but I also felt my dear grandfather standing by me, supporting me as he always did when he was on Earth. It was a moment that will remain etched in my memory forever, and while it was such a painful moment, it was also full of unconditional love, and a deep knowing that what I had just given him was helping.

> **When my dear little man was just ten Earth days old, and still only thirty-six weeks grown, I faced the most frightening and life-changing event of my life.**

The nurses allowed my husband and I to hold our precious boy for just five minutes, just in case he didn't survive the surgery he was about to receive. My baby was about to have open heart surgery to repair not one, but two holes in his heart. The following eight hours were the longest of my life. I wandered around the city like a zombie – not knowing how to feel, what to think, or whether I would be seeing my baby boy alive again. Hundreds of lovely souls on social media – friends, family and members of my Facebook page sent love and healing prayers, but I couldn't bring myself to read them. I was grateful, but it hurt too much.

**I knew that my little boy had
so many people praying for him,
and while part of me had faith
that he would be okay,
I am human after all,
and the pain I felt as a mother
not knowing whether her son
was going to live or die
that day was excruciating.**

Late in the day, when I felt like I was going to be physically sick from waiting to hear whether the surgery was successful or not, I received a message from that same Lightworker friend. She told me that my grandfather had appeared to her in her kitchen while she was making herself something to eat, and he was quite pushy in making sure she passed on the message to me. He told her that he was watching over the surgeons, making sure that they 'did it properly' and that he was with my baby boy throughout the whole ordeal.

**My grandfather wanted me to know that he
was going to be okay. This message was one
that I needed; the only thing that kept me sane
while I waited for that phone call.**

Shortly afterwards, my phone rang and it was the heart surgeon. 'The surgery was successful and we are preparing him for recovery', he said. I wanted to reach down the phone and hug him! The absolute relief I felt at that moment was indescribable, and I felt the presence not only of my beautiful grandfather, but of every single being (on Earth and in Spirit) who had helped heal my son.

Today, my little Heart Warrior is three years old, and while he still loves to hold my hand all the time (understandably), his heart is fully healed – it's as if he never had the problem at all.

As you can imagine, this experience helped me to realise just how real our connection is with Spirit, and to never underestimate the power of prayer, love and healing energy.

I knew when I fell pregnant again just nine months later, that my angel baby was coming back to me, just as I had suspected.

This pregnancy was a breeze – no complications at all, and I knew when my daughter was born 'on time', healthy and oh-so content, that yes, this was her. She had just been waiting for the right time to join me, and she had made room for her older brother to come into our lives first, so that I could awaken in time for her brilliant energy to join us.

This stubborn little Miss is just like me, and was even born with very similar planetary alignments, which explains why we are so alike. She is not even two years old yet, but I already know what she is teaching me. My little 'Queen' (as I call her – I don't like the term 'princess' – she doesn't need saving) is already showing me the parts of myself that I need to allow to shine. She reminds me to regularly reconnect with my own inner child, and to see the world as she does. My daughter is most definitely a very old soul, and it shows in her words and even more so, in her eyes. I know that she is going to make such a difference in this world, and I am so very proud to be her Mumma.

As I said earlier, there are many, many moments during my thirty-seven years of my journey in this lifetime that have helped me to understand my role as a Lightworker, but I believe that my children are the ones who have taught me the most, and continue to do so.

Without them I wouldn't have been pushed to go within, to reach out to Spirit for help and support, or to search for a deeper understanding of life. It is with their help that I have been able to find my true self – my Light self – and why my mission here in this lifetime to help humanity heal is so important.

I am helping to create a better world by raising children who are compassionate, authentic and part of a generation of spiritually awakened souls. For anyone who is a parent, caregiver, works with children, or has an influence on our young generation in any way, please don't ever underestimate the change that you are helping to bring into the world. Our children need to be nurtured and supported to be their true selves; the souls that they have incarnated to be; not who society tries to mold them into.

Children come into this world already full of love, compassion, non-judgement and kindness. If you are playing a part in nurturing these qualities in the children you come into contact with, then you are helping to heal the world.

Namaste, Christie xo

'World peace must develop from inner peace.
Peace is not just mere absence of violence.
Peace is, I think, the manifestation of
human compassion.'

Dalai Lama

Christie Lyons
Christie is a Lightworker, publisher, and writer, and is the founder and director of White Light Universal.

Christie prides herself on being authentic and seeing the light and love in everyone she meets, and this shines through in both the healing and guidance she provides for her clients, as well as helping writers' and artists' publishing dreams come true.

Her passions are writing, mental health, children's rights, and playing a part in healing humanity.

More about Christie
Website:
www.whitelightuniversal.com.au
Facebook:
www.facebook.com/whitelightforthesoul
www.facebook.com/whitelightpublishinghouse
Instagram:
www.instagram.com/whitelightuniversal
Pinterest:
www.au.pinterest.com/whitelightsoul

Welcome Back, *Light*

By Lauren Kelly

I was a little taken aback when Christie asked me to submit a story for this beautiful compilation. I had it firmly set in my mind that a Lightworker is someone who does spiritual work, a psychic who helps people connect with lost loved ones or perhaps a Reiki Master ... you get the picture. Whilst I believe we all have the ability to connect with spirit, I have managed to block my connection. I am on a journey to open up to all that is locked away but, that is a story for another time. I told Christie I didn't see myself as a Lightworker. My beautiful daughter raised her eyebrows at me and asked, 'What about all you do for homeless people; and how about what you do for the kids in Nepal?' Well, that certainly got me thinking more about the definition of a Lightworker. What a beautiful feeling it was when it really dawned on me. I am a Lightworker, yep, I am most definitely a Lightworker and this is a little about my path to finding my light and how I share it with the world.

I've never really been a religious person. I didn't, and still don't think a great deal of organised religion. I did believe in God, though. My faith in Him was seriously damaged when my best friend, Jenny, was tragically killed in a car accident. I was filled with so much anger and pain.

I had the driver to direct my anger at and in the depths of my despair, I told myself, 'God can't be real; there is no way He would leave two young children without a Mummy!' And dammit, if he did exist he also left me without my beautiful best friend so, that would also make him partly responsible for my pain.

**So, what to do?
Stop believing in God,
or blame Him for the pain
He had allowed into my life.
I decided I could get along
just fine without my faith.**

I was six months pregnant with my son when Jen passed. A few months after my beautiful baby boy entered the world, we headed off for a family getaway. We were going to the lovely country town of Echuca. We didn't have the reasonably straight stretches of the Princes Highway to take us all the way through, back then. The old back roads weren't too bad, although there were quite a few bends to negotiate. I was driving my car with my now ex-husband in the passenger seat and baby Ian was safely tucked up in his capsule. Christie was travelling with her beloved grandparents in their car. I had only had my license for a few years but I was a reasonably confident driver. I was cruising along one of the straight stretches, and when it was safe to do so, I was sticking to the speed limit of 100 kph. All of a sudden, I had the most overwhelming feeling, I knew if I put my hand over the back, Jenny would have taken hold of it. I also felt I'd have seen her sitting there if I looked in the rear-view mirror. I didn't look for fear of being startled and having an accident. I slowed down to not much more than a crawl; and just as my ex-husband was asking me what I was doing, there was a loud bang. One of my tyres had blown out and it gave me one heck of a fright. There is absolutely no doubt in my mind that Jen was sitting in the back seat that day. I may have been a confident driver, but I'm quite sure I would have freaked out; and most probably had a serious accident if I hadn't slowed down. Although I have never again felt her presence as strongly as I did that day, I never doubt that my beautiful friend is always close by.

This incident did not restore my faith in God; that was to be many years in the future before that would happen.

After breaking up with my partner of almost ten years, he made the decision to end his life. Rather than working through my grief and dealing with this tragedy, I escaped by partying as often and as hard as I could. After a few years, and some additional and particularly nasty things life had to throw at me and my family, depression set in. Great time to see a counsellor and deal with everything, right? Nope, anti-depressants and more partying seemed to be far easier. The anti-depressants helped me to think rationally and I was having a lot of fun partying which I thought was helping to keep the emotions locked away.

There were some rather dark moments during that time where anti-depressants couldn't touch the depths of despair I felt; I just immersed myself into an online world and used that as yet another form of escape.

Studying tarot – at first with a long-distance teacher and then with my daughter – I had to look deep within as I journeyed through each card. Not only did this lead me to finally process and release all of the dark emotions I had buried for so long, I found this overwhelming love and compassion for myself; something I hadn't shown myself in who knows how long, if ever. I like to think I have always been kind, caring and compassionate to others, but I most certainly hadn't been nice to me. This was such a wonderfully healing experience; looking deep within my soul had helped me to learn that I deserved to be loved; most importantly, I deserved to be loved by myself.

Once I let love and light into the very core of my being, I was able to look at all of the tough experiences I had been through and accept them as lessons.

These lessons had shaped me into the person I was always meant to be, the person I am now. There was another light shining oh so brightly and joined with my own. With that light came another love, a love that I was finally ready to accept once more.

God hadn't been planning all of these horrible events to dish out to me. He didn't turn his back on me in my hour of need.

He patiently and lovingly waited for me to learn my lessons, knowing I would awaken when the time was right.

I was working at a corporate job in the city at this time. I always thought I'd hate being caught up in the rush hours; I didn't hate it all, I loved it. I could see past the crazy hustle and bustle, I could see people, so many people. They come from every walk of life you can imagine, well dressed corporates, stylish retail workers, shoppers; people from such a diverse range of cultures. I'm sure many of them thought I was nuts walking around with a big smile on my face. I just wanted to get as many of them as possible to smile back. At first, I would count the smiles I got back each day and try to increase the number I got the next day; it wasn't long before the number didn't matter – each and every smile was a gift being returned to me for the smile I had given. I also realised that a smile not being returned didn't mean mine wasn't received gratefully, these people could have been going through their own set of issues, or maybe just having a shitty day. I've always said smiling is contagious and I wanted to infect everyone I could. Even on days when I didn't feel so happy, I'd get my smile out and share it. It wasn't a fake smile, not by a long shot. On these days, each smile I got back was like a soothing lotion, and it was also a reminder of the value of that oh-so-simple act.

I had started to feel differently about the way I was going about life, and felt a great need to share my abundance of love and compassion with the world.

Before I worked in the city, I had absolutely no idea that so many people were experiencing homelessness here. Yes, I was actually naïve enough to think we didn't have much of a homeless problem here in Australia; certainly not in my Melbourne. I did see the odd person sitting on a street corner, but the few I saw on my way to and from work certainly didn't indicate just how big the issue is. I avoided any form of news back then, I much preferred to keep as much sadness out of my little bubble as I could. In fact, I didn't watch television for more than ten years. That way, I wouldn't even see a news bulletin. If I wanted to know what the weather was like, I either looked out the window or asked my friend Google to give me a forecast. That being the case, it was no surprise I hadn't heard about a murder that happened in the city.

A few years ago, I received an email at work about a rally being held in the city. There wasn't a great deal of information, but it did say that the rally had something to do with homelessness. I researched a little more about the rally and was horrified to learn that it was being held in memory of Morgan Wayne 'Mouse' Perry, who had been brutally murdered in Enterprize Park, just across the river from where I worked. It was definitely time for me to stop hiding away from the news. I knew I needed to pop my protective bubble and let the world in. I knew if I didn't start finding out what was going on in the world, I wouldn't know what I could do to help. I felt an overwhelming need to do something; I didn't have any answers on how homelessness could be ended, I barely knew anything about it and its existence in my beautiful city. I just knew this was a place where my love and compassion could be shared. I wanted to know why this man who had been murdered was homeless, I also wondered just how many homeless people we actually have in this city. So, I attended the 'Rally for Mouse', I listened intently to all of the speakers as they told about the extent of people experiencing homelessness in Melbourne, many of whom were living right across from where I worked. I cried as I listened to Michele Perry, Morgan's sister as she shared stories of her beautiful younger brother and how he had changed from a beautiful fun-loving young boy after being abused.

> **I walked away with a firm resolve that I would do my best to make a difference to people experiencing homelessness.**

The next morning, I stopped at the supermarket on my way to work to buy a few simple items: a small bottle of juice, some fruit and a couple of other food items. Instead of catching the tram from the station, I walked through Enterprize Park and went to one of the pylons where I could see a young man sleeping. I didn't want to wake him, but I did want to make sure the goodies were close enough so he'd see them when he did awaken. I gave it a gentle throw, thinking it wouldn't make much noise, but it did; it landed with a thud. The young man almost jumped right out of his bed, and I nearly jumped out of my skin. I let him know I'd just dropped off some food and practically ran away. After this, I dropped food off to the same young man on a regular basis. After a few visits we began chatting and I learned from my new friend Sam, that very few people would give rough sleepers the time of day and quite often, people would shout abuse at them or suggest they get a job.

> **It became apparent very quickly that we live in an incredibly judgemental society.**

Another thing that struck home was the absolute lack of awareness around homelessness. Sure, my bubble I'd been hiding away in had made sure I had no idea, but nobody I spoke to had the slightest idea of just how many people were experiencing homelessness.

One of our homelessness services here, Melbourne City Mission, holds an event called Sleep at the 'G to raise funds for Youth Homelessness. This sounded like a fun way to help raise awareness and money at the same time. I decided I needed a team name so I asked Sam to help me come up with a meaningful name. He asked me if I had heard of Mouse, and I learned that he and Sam had been good mates. Sam asked if I could use his mate's name somehow. Since Sam was now living in Enterprize Park, and Morgan, aka Mouse had been murdered in the same park, we came up with Mouse's Enterprize. Sam asked me if I had a sleeping bag to use for the event and told me I was more than welcome to borrow his. Here he was, sleeping under a railway bridge, with little more than a sleeping bag to his name, and he was genuinely happy to lend it to me. I had already decided that I'd buy a new sleeping bag and donate it to a homeless person afterwards, but I certainly wouldn't leave someone sleeping rough with no sleeping bag on a cold autumn night.

The person who was meant to attend the event with me decided not to go and since I now had a spare ticket, I asked Sam if he'd like to go with me. Team Mouse's Enterprize raised just over $2,000 for Melbourne City Mission and we had a great night at the event. I met so many amazing people, some of whom were volunteers for a grass roots organisation called The Big Umbrella, a group who provide meals in the city for people experiencing homelessness. Sam and I caught a train back into the city the next morning and had a cuppa whilst sitting at the pylons in Enterprize Park.

> **It was quite a cold morning and I felt terrible that I could go home to my little unit and have a real sleep in a warm bed, whilst Sam stayed in the park next to the river with his sleeping bag.**

One of the donations our team received was from Michele Perry. I was thrilled to read the lovely message Michele left with her donation. I thought more on how we had used Mouse's Enterprize as our team name for Sleep at the 'G and decided to get in touch with Michele and ask her if it would be okay to create a Facebook page with the same name. I explained to Michele that I'd like to keep her brother's memory alive by creating more awareness about homelessness. Since I had learned about so many grass roots organisations who do so much to support people who are sleeping rough, I felt I could also assist by promoting awareness about their existence. So, Mouse's Enterprize page was created and all funds I help to raise for homelessness is always done in honour of Morgan Wayne 'Mouse' Perry. To date, Team Mouse's Enterprize has proudly raised over $6,000 for Melbourne City Mission's Sleep at the 'G event and will continue to attend and raise funds each year.

I visited the park often over the next few months and got to know a few of the guys. Sam and his mate Woodsy were the main two I spoke to and I built up quite a friendship with them. I bought them a little camp stove and took in a few basic cooking utensils. The homelessness services don't provide food seven days a week anyway and depending on who was around in the park, the guys were careful about leaving their few belongings to go to where the food is served. I would sometimes make a huge pot of vegetable soup, grab some fresh bread and spend a Sunday afternoon at the pylons. Some nights I'd just drop by for a chat with the guys after work. Occasionally, some of the outreach team from The Big Umbrella would stop by and check on how the guys were all doing and drop off various items, including toiletries or clothing. TBU provide meals in the city a couple of nights each week for those in need and also team up with another crew on Christmas Day.

I felt like my life finally had purpose.

I wasn't ending homelessness, but I sure as heck was making a difference to some people who were experiencing it. I made up a swag of Christmas stockings with a few goodies, and much needed items such as socks and toiletries. I packed them up in my little shopping jeeps with some cold bottles of fresh water and headed off with Sam to hand them out to some of our friends on the street.

Such a small contribution was quite clearly making a huge difference. The huge smiles I got from each person brought so much joy to my heart.

I no longer work in the city, and don't get as much time to volunteer with some of the awesome crews I've met along the way, Anonymous X, From Us 2 You Melbourne, to mention just a couple. I will continue to promote awareness and do what I can to make a difference; whenever and wherever I'm able. There are so many pathways into homelessness; domestic violence, sexual abuse, mental health issues and loss of income are but a few of them. Judging people experiencing homelessness does absolutely nothing to help. Everyone has a different story; that girl sitting on the corner who looks like she taking drugs, she quite possibly is. She may have started using after suffering years of physical or emotional abuse. I know drugs are not the answer, but hey, I'm not living in her head, so I have no right to decide what she should or shouldn't do. Maybe she's just tired and hungry because she has to sleep with one eye open every night; and the money she got from begging, well it's that time of the month and she doesn't want to resort to stealing. What would you choose? Food or feminine hygiene products?

Whatever the case may be, I choose to see a human being; a beautiful soul who has lost their way and needs some love and light.

Some days, just saying hello gives her all the love she needs to get through the day. She knows somebody has acknowledged her existence. She is no longer invisible.

I have certainly learned the incredible value of even the smallest of kind acts. By making a difference to one person, we create change in the whole world. Never underestimate just what a simple hello or smile can do for someone. Saying hello to that girl just might shine enough light on her heart and help her decide she can actually get through another day, or maybe find herself closer to the answers to her problems. Love is incredible, and believe it or not, it is even more incredible when you give that gift to yourself. It creates a beautiful ripple effect and gives you even more love to share with others; and the urge to share becomes overwhelming.

That's okay though, because the well never has to run dry, never!

Lauren Kelly
Lauren is the proud mother of two adult children, and grandmother to seven beautiful grandchildren.

After recently leaving the corporate world, Lauren now works alongside her daughter Christie for White Light Universal and loves it! Lauren is passionate about helping the less fortunate, particularly people experiencing homelessness.

Her goal is to play a huge part in healing humanity by sharing and encouraging love.

www.whitelightuniversal.com.au
www.facebook.com/whitelightpublishinghouse

To find out more about Mouse's Enterprize:
www.facebook.com/MousesEnterprize

Do you want to find out more
about being a Lightworker?

Visit us at
www.whitelightuniversal.com.au
for more information

Someone asked me,
'What is your religion?'

I replied,
'All paths that lead to the light.'

'Healers are spiritual warriors
who have found the courage
to defeat the darkness of their souls.

Awakening and rising from the
depths of their deepest fears,
like a Phoenix rising from the ashes.

Reborn with a wisdom and
strength that creates a light
that shines bright enough to help,
encourage, and inspire others
out of their own darkness.'

Melanie Koulouris

Also available
http://www.whitelightpublishing.com.au/

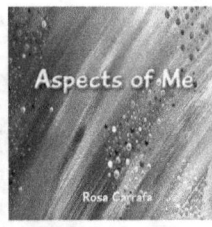

Coming Soon

Joy
Michelle George

Weight Loss in Middle Life:
How to get out of the Diet Trap
Jane Turner

The Revelation Trilogy
Matt Eastwood

Crystal Alchemy
Lani Sharp

Tarot: An Astrological Journey
Lani Sharp

Angelical Wisdoms
Julia Van Der Sluys

Wake Up
Leanne Magoulias

Return of the Morning Star
Tracey Madigan

Food and Wisdom to Nourish the Soul
Michael Moir

How to Survive a Miscarriage:
A Guide for Women, their Partners, Friends & Families
Karin Holmes

Divine Zodiac Messages
Lani Sharp

One's Love
Tara Spackman

Teal the Magic Fairy
Tahel Berkman

Self Discovery Inspirational Cards
Tegan Neville

Fair Dinkum Aussie Poetry
Shauna Norman

To keep updated on new releases, go to
www.whitelightpublishing.com.au

www.ingramcontent.com/pod-product-compliance
Lightning Source LLC
Chambersburg PA
CBHW071905290426
44110CB00013B/1290